Enjoying Maine's Islands

Remembering

BESSIE HANSON GIBSON
and
JOHN EDWARD GIBSON

Other Books by John Gibson

50 Hikes in Maine

Walking the Maine Coast

Go Light

Walking the New England Coast

50 Hikes in Coastal and Southern Maine

Maine's Most Scenic Roads:
25 Routes Off the Beaten Path

New Hampshire's Most Scenic Roads:
22 Routes Off the Beaten Path

The Traveler's Guide to the Most Scenic
Roads In Massachusetts

Weekend Walks on the New England Coast

Rivers of Memory:
A Journey on Maine's Historic Midcoast Waterways

JOHN GIBSON

Enjoying Maine's Islands

THE ESSENTIAL GUIDE TO 15 DESTINATIONS YOU CAN REACH BY FERRY

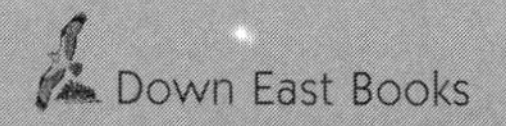

FRONT COVER PHOTOGRAPHS

Grindle Point Light, Islesboro (John Gibson)

Cliff Island ferry (© Charles Feil)

BACK COVER PHOTOGRAPHS

by John Gibson

Photographs by the author unless otherwise noted.

ISBN (10-digit): 0-89272-677-6

ISBN (13-digit): 978-089272-677-6

Design by Lurelle Cheverie

Printed at Versa Press, E. Peoria, Ill.

2 4 5 3 1

Down East Books

A division of Down East Enterprise, Inc.

Publisher of *Down East*, the Magazine of Maine

Book orders: 1-800-685-7962

www.downeastbooks.com

Library of Congress Cataloging-in-Publication Data

Gibson, John, 1940-

Enjoying Maine's islands : the essential guide to

15 destinations you can reach by ferry / John Gibson.

p. cm.

ISBN 0-89272-677-6 (trade pbk.)

1. Islands—Maine—Guidebooks. 2. Maine—Guidebooks.

3. Atlantic Coast(Me.)—Guidebooks. 4. Bays—Maine—

Guidebooks. 5. Ferries—Maine—Guidebooks. I. Title.

F27.A19G53 2005

917.4104'44—dc22

2005014880

Contents

THE MAINE COAST

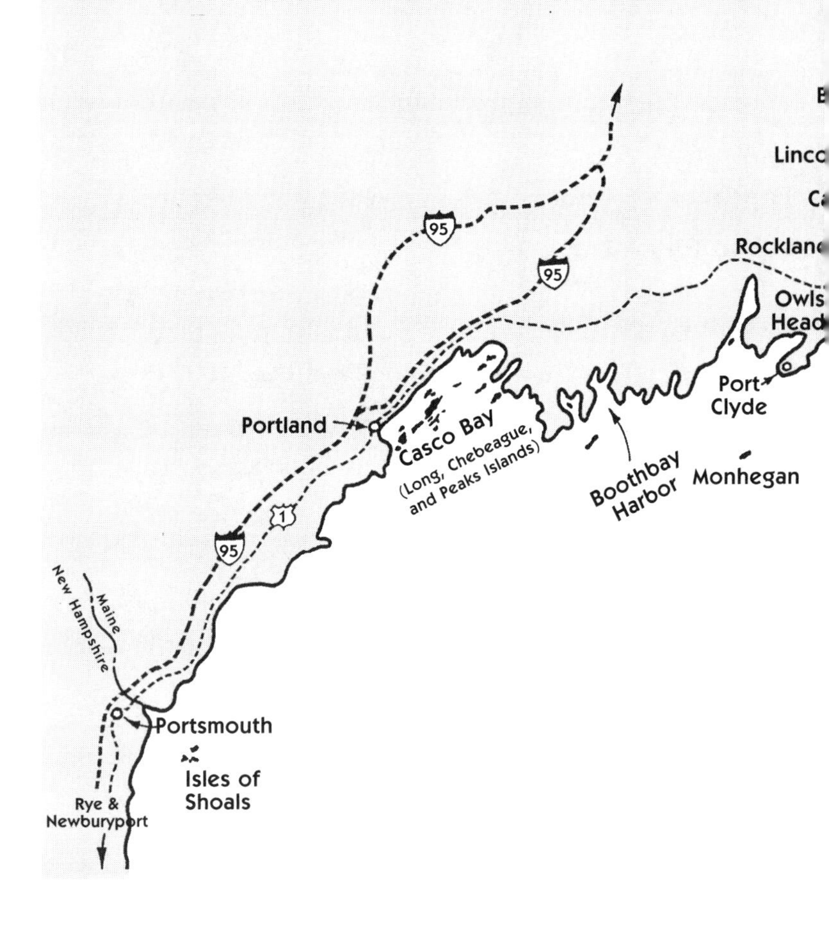

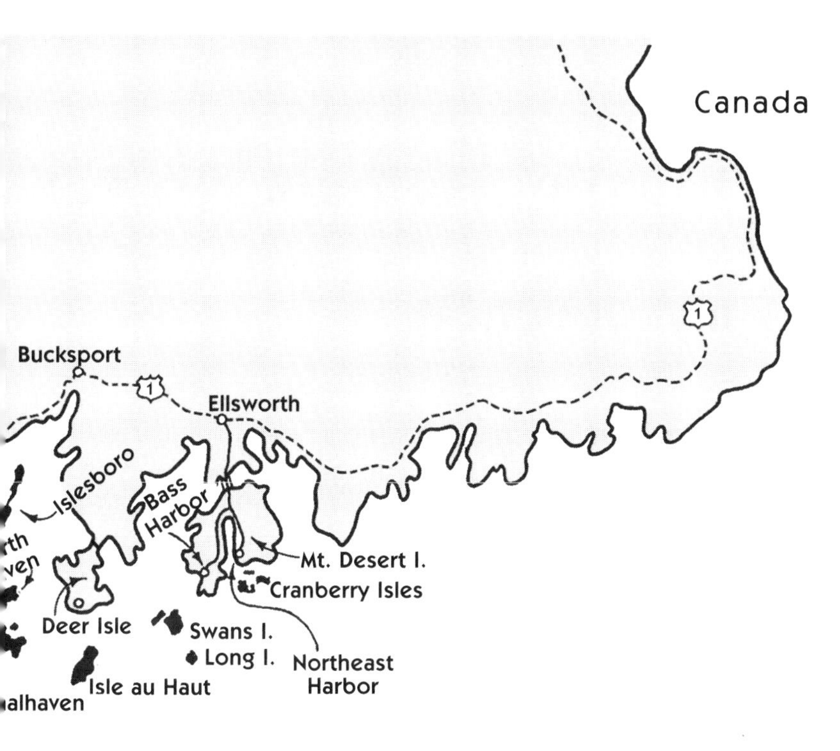
Canada
Bucksport
Ellsworth
Islesboro
Bass Harbor
Mt. Desert I.
Cranberry Isles
Deer Isle
Swans I.
Long I.
Northeast Harbor
Isle au Haut

N

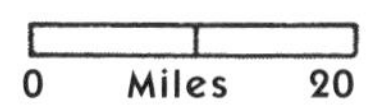
0 Miles 20

Enjoying Maine's Islands

INTRODUCTION

If you long for islands, there is hope. Your hunger is as basic as such appetites are wont to be; you have a survival sense that says the organized world must be left behind for a day, a week, or longer while you are reconstituted, made whole. You are not alone in this. Others, small handfuls of them here and there, have gone before, and, when you come aboard, they will admit you to the healing outposts they have prepared. Do not expect to be coddled.

Maine's Atlantic islands have for centuries supported a way of life like no other. These islands served as fishing and birding outposts for the Northeast's aboriginal peoples well before Norse explorations, and Europeans fished here long prior to the establishment of mainland settlements. Maine's islands also became points of exchange for farming and various coastal trades. They were and are useful places stationed at various crossroads of shorewise and open-ocean traffic. Tenuous communities arose, their way of life like no opulent mainland existence, the hard, primitive comforts of island life similar only to other northern island cultures at distant corners of the earth.

Each island is precious territory, but real enough. There is nothing romantic here except as you make it. Maine's islands have become, more or less by accident, part of those few remaining outposts of separation in this world that offer relief from the sheer craziness of contemporary life. It does not matter how well you think you live; islands are a special tonic, if given to stubborn simplicity. Island people know this, and they expect you to join in the spirit of offshore life, too. Islanders are polite and helpful, but do not expect them to be delirious with joy at your arrival. These are practical outposts, people busy with earning a living in a distant place.

Maine boasts a variety of offshore places, many totally private, hidden, and owned by magnates with unpronounceable names from elsewhere. I have visited a few of these by invitation, but they are not what this book is about. You will find introduced here those island places that are still linked tenuously with the larger world and where, as of the moment, the inhabitants smile at you and make you welcome. These are islands, among the many, that you can get to without necessarily owning a yacht. (Mine is in pawn at the moment.) They range from large, settled islands in Casco Bay such as Peaks, Long, or Chebeague—which, when their occupants look to the distant southwest, reveal the skyline of Portland, the state's largest city—to that group of islands (or shoals) to the south, owned jointly by Maine and New Hampshire off the Piscataqua, where pirates cavorted and ghosts still walk in the wake of tragedy. Farther north, off the Midcoast, lie islands such as Matinicus and Monhegan, each with its strong links to fishing and lobstering going back centuries. Or Swans and its little neighbor Frenchboro, lost in a cold sea southeast of Mount Desert. In between there are still others, each with merits of its own.

Maine's Atlantic islands come in a variety of textures and sizes, though there are some general conventions. Philip Conkling, in his indispensable *Islands in Time*, has noted: "Maine's islands come in one of two shapes. They are either long and narrow like the islands of Casco and Muscongus Bays, or they are rounded and domed like Mount Desert, Deer Isle, Swans, Isle au Haut, Vinalhaven and Beals. . . ." Whatever their shapes and sizes, many have earned a name, often arising from some local incident or practice or convention, that captures a historic essence, idiosyncrasy, or use.

Thus, we find off both Brooklin and the Isles of Shoals *two* islands named Smuttynose, elsewhere at least *two* Pound of Tea Islands, and off Portland and Sorrento *two* Junk o' Pork isles. Bombazeen lies off Harpswell, Killickstone off Bristol, and East Brown Cow off Phippsburg. Aunt Mollie rests off Penobscot, the Hypocrites near Boothbay, Two Bush off Harpswell, and the *two* Cuckolds off Portland and near Damariscove. Popes Folly takes the tides near Lubec, Jordans Delight rides off Millbridge, and Sow and Pigs looks on Freeport. And then one discovers solitary isles such as Big Hen and Rabbits Ear. The titles are almost limitless. Nomenclature aside, these seaborne places are worthy because of their beauty, their connections with a vanishing mode of living, their varied history in the early settlement of America, and their feeling of separateness whether near to shore or in deep.

Native Americans came first to these places, fishing and hunting on the islands, often camping here in summer to escape inland swarms of insects. They were the easternmost migrants of an Asiatic group of Beringian travelers of uncertain origin and, perhaps, also of a lost, primitive culture in southwestern France. A native presence in Maine has existed for at least twelve thousand years, some recent estimates regarding coastal and island settlements farther south are even more remote in time.

Norse exploration probably brought longboats into these waters around 1000 C.E. Maine's offshore islands were once a point of first reference on the maps of many European explorers and merchant adventurers. Continental fishermen commenced journeying to the region in the 1400s. Eager claimants followed thereafter, backed by London and Paris merchant fortunes and royal decrees. A troubled and contentious dance arose in the discovery years of European and Indian interaction, both alongshore and on the islands. European arrivals missed few opportunities to exploit Indian trust. Numerous kidnappings and swindles destroyed the initially passive Indian response to visitation, and natives began to reply in kind. European predation on Indian lands grew, sometimes leading to outright murder, and the New England–wide hostilities that began with King Philip's War were ignited. Occasionally, natives had the last laugh.

Historical documents confirm at least one island encounter between Europeans and Indians that was expressive of the moment. The May 1524 diary entries of the Italian explorer Giovanni Verrazano relate the rocky road of early contact. Verrazano had turned his *La Dauphine* north and was working his way up Maine's Midcoast in the company of islands, bound homeward for France. After initial wariness, an arrangement to trade was made with a band of natives along an island headland. The Indians lowered baskets of their produce and wares to Verrazano's boats, and then hauled items exchanged back up to their perch. Besides gaining something fresh to eat, the explorers were interested in taking home artifacts illustrative of discovery. The Indians preferred metal knives and fishhooks.

When Verrazano hoisted anchor and set sail again, he looked for a gracious signal of safe departure from the natives, but received, instead, a different kind of farewell. Scanning the cliffs with his glass, he noted that his band of Indians were laughing merrily on the island tops and making a variety of obscene gestures. All had turned their backs to the sea and had cheerfully exposed their bare backsides to his offended gaze, each in a frenzy of hooting and hollering. Natives 1, Explorers 0. Verrazano made a note of this insult, and commented of the encounter that this was "a place of bad people."

The coastal islands of Maine are the result of an ancient geological shell game. Their underlayment is either metamorphic rock on the south coast, which extends inland under river valleys such as the Kennebec, or igneous, granitic plutons farther north. Their sculpted terrain and vegetation yield a unique, well-salted character distinctive on the Atlantic coast.

The islands, like some of Maine's coastal bays, show the effect of glaciation. Twenty-three to twenty-one thousand years ago, the coast of Maine lay under a mile-thick sheet of ice that gradually receded, eventually melting away completely some eleven thousand years ago. The glacier left its mark. The weight of this great sheet of ice first depressed the coastal zone, and then scrubbed the landforms beneath it as the ice moved forward. Maine's coastal plain rebounded somewhat as the ice withdrew, but the incalculable gallons of melted water released across the northern hemisphere flooded these regions and adjacent river valleys. Standing above today's raised sea levels, Maine's sea islands remain as markers of an earlier coastline. These ledgy mounds today support unique communities and repay inspection, each a fine monument to isolation. And, exploring these islands on foot, you will witness here and there the marks, noted earlier, left by the passage of glacial ice over their surfaces. Ledges on high ground now well offshore display these interesting, abraded striations, signs of glacial scrubbing in a variety of island places. Subsequent weathering has created the thin soils that have very slowly built up on these offshore rock piles; wind and birds have seeded them for millennia.

With an increase in coastal immersion occurring today as global warming melts glaciers and polar regions worldwide, Maine's islands are slowly becoming farther offshore and thus more remote, a situation that will not disappoint some islanders. Coastal immersion potentially will bring island immersion, too, and certain low-lying islands have been given something to think about. With remoteness, past or present, comes danger, and Maine islands are historically awash in stories of shipwreck and disaster that attest to this reality. Rising seas are simply one more addition to this reality. As Philip Conkling has reminded, "Part of the reason Maine islands do not have more inhabitants frequenting their shores is that the seas around them and the airs over them can be, like a wild animal you have found and made into a pet, very unpredictable. One moment sleek and tame, another wild, ungrateful, even brutal."

Many of Maine's offshore islands were logged in the earlier years of settlement, their timber used for building, cordwood, and cooperage. Islands that were cleared later offered pasturage, and sheep farming occurred on those isles well suited. In the mid- to late 1800s there were two thousand sheep grazing on North Haven and twelve hundred on Monhegan. Smaller numbers grazed on islands scattered throughout the Gulf of Maine. Remnants of this pocket industry still exist. One is reminded of Peter Ralston's much-exhibited photographs of sheep being ferried to island grazing in recent years. It is a tradition worth preserving. Maine's at-sea islands are stopping-off places for all manner of avian life, and the seas around the islands support varying species of seals and passing whales. Fox, bear, mink, raccoon, deer in abundance, and, perhaps, the rare moose occupy many islands. Small migrating and seasonally nesting birds flit from isle to isle. Seabirds make their lives around the islands in great numbers, and populations of large predators such as hawks are often best sighted during spring and fall migrations from offshore. The high ground of Monhegan sees great rafts of bird-watchers arrive for autumn hawk-watching each year. Just as regularly, the buteos and accipiters arrive on schedule to observe the bird-watchers. Some offshore places, such as Matinicus Rock, have been protected, and one of Maine's colonies of attractive puffins prospers there. In summer, a walk along the paths of a wooded island treats the wanderer to dense cadenzas of birdsong, each intensely available to the ear above the flat acoustics of the surrounding sea.

• • • •

Enjoying Maine's Islands

As much as wildlife, island stone and vegetation delight the eye. Island geography and isolation always offer something different as to flavor when compared with the mainland. The real merits of islands lie, as I've suggested, in their separateness. Little can be said to fully explain this attraction except to observe that as mainland life grows more intolerable across the globe, islands become more obviously places of refuge where one tangibly senses *difference.*

There are islands where I have spent foggy weekends off the coast of Maine that effectively erased all sense of baneful television news, a crumbling stock market, and backed-up traffic on expressways. The notable absence of a brightly lit McDonald's just left of the bait shed is reassuring. Very scarce on islands, the perpetual hype and sales mentality of the mainland is refreshing in its absence. One realizes that much of one's everyday mainland life is merely media noise, blaring, shouting, coaxing, inveigling, threatening. Walking out toward the cliffs in embracing fog only to be suddenly greeted by an islander as he or she emerges from the thick, salted air is an unexpected pleasure. And then, more silence. One dares the larger world to make its trivialities felt here.

These islands, meant to be experienced as such, do not yield easily to demands for the comforts of suburbia, the entertainments of noisy cities, or the motorized or electronic conveniences familiar to people who are strangers to walking. Day-trippers,

Islands can serve as a base for kayak journeys
Photograph of author by Dianna Rust

descending from the ferry, will enjoy their island visit most if they come prepared to scale rough ledge and gravel roads. Islanders, the genuine article, dress for the life they live. Making do, even a kind of primitiveness, are an island's best defense against characterless modernity. Visitors do well to keep this in mind. There is, after all, something contradictory about deliberately making your way offshore only to bring the detritus of mainland culture with you. Islands are places of improvisation and should be left so.

Maine islands boast a certain exceptionality as to appearance. Though in tropical southern Maine, islands may sport the deciduous growth common on the mainland, as you work northward the vegetation and its visible underlayment begin to change. Rock and ledge show themselves more and more along island peripheries. Dark groves of conifers dominate. Ledge, seen from a boat, reveals itself to be just under the surface of everything, forcing you to revise your sense of what is stood upon. There is a coldness, too, about such a landscape, a hard, unyielding beauty. Few other island places on the North American continent appear quite as do these Maine islands—their mysterious metallic greenness, their ageless rocky footings, their shaded glades of mossy stone. If you take a boat or paddle a kayak through the chain of islands from Stonington to Isle au Haut you will see what I mean. *Separateness*, I think, in all the keen forms in which you can experience it, were it to have a particular color, texture, and shape, would look like these islands.

Without explanation, human artifacts crop up here and there, sometimes as if growing from the very ground. They *appear* to be of human origin, at least. The late Maine author and humorist John Gould once puzzled over the strange stone circle found on Damariscove Island. It is a stone wall in a circle, and John asked why in the world and who in the world would build such a thing, given the extensive manual labor and mechanical ingenuity involved. After all, what needed to be fenced out or in, he inquired. From whom did islanders, there since the 1500s, need to be shielded? The stone circle, John noted, pre-dated anybody we know of by an eternity—the Norse, Italians, and Portuguese, Mr. Columbus, the Phoenicians, the fanciful "Pilgrims."

How to explain these things? Or the writings on rock at Monhegan? Perhaps the work of those who came before *anyone* arrived from the Atlantic or Mediterranean world? I had wanted to lend John an essay on Dun Aengus and its situation on the Aran Islands off the west coast of Ireland, but he, perhaps, was already aware of it. There is an ancient stone circle there, too, backing up to the sea. And then there are the eerie ghost ships that navigate among these islands. Unexplainable shapes floating on oily surf—silent, uncrewed, adrift.

Maine's offshore island communities enliven the imagination because so many of the convenient, drugging rituals of everyday life as experienced elsewhere are inconvenient, cranky, difficult, or absent at sea. Out beyond, you must be creative. Improvise. Pay attention. For example, islands are places where you do not trade in or sell your car; you hide it in the bushes and forget it until the engine or transmission becomes useful for some other purpose. Venerable cars go unregistered, left to rust in the scrub until called upon to roll briefly, doing some odd manner of work. Sometimes they are merely engine and frame, an old wooden chair lashed to the chassis for the driver to sit on. There are few objects that do not have a new, potential utility on an island, and materials such as sheet metal or old lumber are hoarded in the event of some unexpected future need. You find occasional heaps of this stuff submitting to rust or rot in hidden corners of island woods.

When you go to church on these isles, the reverend may arrive by boat, render his sermon, and then turn his craft for another island destination. Peddlers, tinkers, and cobblers formerly came to harbor, anchored, and provided their services for a few days, then moved on to the next island. Shopping today often means getting a mainland grocery to put up your order and then send it out by boat or plane. Photographer and writer Charles Pratt captured these unconventionalities in word and picture in his *Here on the Island*, a compelling portrait of an anonymous isle that many assume is Isle au Haut. Pratt's photographs fittingly capture the eccentricity of island life and the ingenuity of survival in such outposts. Living offshore is not for the helpless.

The social climate of Maine's offshore islands usually runs to complexity, past and present existing simultaneously. Architectural historian Robert Millen has written of his favorite island off Newfoundland that every fence, rock, house, field, shed, marsh, cultivated plot, or bait wharf has a convoluted and tangled history of use going back generations. So it is with many of Maine's offshore outposts. Families become dominant and then decline. Others arrive and establish themselves. They intermarry. Property moves from family to family and sometimes back again. People retire and decide to move ashore. Boats are built, repaired, or rebuilt. This timeless pattern may lose its way on Maine's islands as fewer people fish or lobster, as island life becomes less tenable for families, and as the declining economy of fishing falters. For now it remains part of the offshore road map.

A "good" island is one with a diverse group of people, those young and old, with a variety of skills, of varying family size and differing purpose. Islands with children mean that the school is kept open. The one-room schoolhouse is still found on coastal islands, its future ever uncertain. An open school often means that other services are kept available, some money comes into the community, and children continue to have experience of island life. A variety of skills fosters the notion of people combining talents and helping out one another. Living and working on an island demand self-sufficiency of every sort, and extra skilled hands are welcome, even crucial. There is no electrician or plumber just up the highway. You make do when the nearest hardware store is twenty miles away over rough water. A mixture of young and old on an island brings the generations together and reminds us of why people chose islands in the first place. Stories keep some of the young offshore, rather than bolting for the often toxic jobs of modern urban life.

As it becomes more difficult to produce a living offshore, some Maine islands have seen residents depart, schools close, and ferry service dwindle.

More island children board out, oldsters leave to go ashore permanently, and the affluent from elsewhere buy up island property. Newcomers rarely are content to live as closely and simply as old islanders did, and many build large monuments in the form of oversized, ever-extending houses. New arrivals from suburbia expect services that aren't logically available. Those who demand all manner of comforts and entertainments find eventually that islands aren't their cup of tea. Occupation of residences becomes merely seasonal, and then only occasional seasons, and then not at all. In the meantime, the island economy is short the family that once lived in the

Isle au Haut

house that once was small. Their skills and interest in community are gone, too. Their children will know only the mainland. On at least some islands, there are two cultures, traditional and in-migrant upscale. The phenomenon appears to be spreading; one wonders if this is the island future.

An egregious example of in-comer attempts to suburbanize Maine's islands occurred not long ago way down east at Beals. This island and its cross-channel opposite, Jonesport, are fishing communities that go way back to the nation's beginnings. The first Beal family arrived in 1765, putting down roots on what had been earlier called Little Wass Island. Stories tell of how one Beals fisherman of extraordinary strength is rumored to have single-handedly taken on a sloop of British regulars who were patrolling the area during the Revolution. The redcoats launched a longboat and approached the man who, instead of running, turned his boat and rammed them. Grabbing hold of the longboat's gunnels, this Beals fellow furiously rocked and hammered until the longboat took on water and then tipped, nearly sending the alarmed British into the frigid current. Beals and Jonesport people go their own way, fish, keep to themselves, and live the traditional coast and island life. Always have.

But, as I was saying, even the easternmost coast and islands have begun to see new arrivals, those from the more affluent territories who want to own a chunk of waterside in this fabled country. Thus, large, newly built houses have begun to dot the shorefront in places even as remote as Beals. Recently, several of the owners of these castles complained to the town that noises were waking them early each morning and at other inconvenient times. They demanded that whoever was making the racket be ordered to stop. Right now. Maine television reporters trotted down east to cover the story.

The sounds, of course, were made by local fishermen, getting their boats ready before sunrise and then heading up or down channel to go to work. Inmigrants tend sometimes to overlook the fact that Maine has a working coast, that people fish here, and that boats leave early to haul. (The assumption of some is, perhaps, that fish and lobster spawn in supermarkets.) It so happens that Beals fishermen tend to haul on the tides. The eight- or ten-knot currents that hurtle through Moosabec Reach produce thirty-foot tides with which one does not argue. In such a neighborhood, one hauls when things are a little less bothersome, low slack and high slack. Coastal Maine people have always deferred to the tide.

News reports said that now Beals and other island and coastal communities have of necessity taken to publishing brochures that are handed out with a smile to would-be relocatees. These brochures remind, in essence, that these are real places, with real people, working real jobs tied to the sea, and if you can't live with that, you should not plan on settling. One Beals lobsterman told a reporter, "They come in here, find it attractive, build a big house, and then want everything changed to make it just like the place they came from."

Still, one finds those little moments of fortuity when a vote is cast for the traditional island way of life. A group of island players led by a talented Broadway producer, himself an island resident, produce a celebration of this way of life and take it to acclaim in New York. Another island says good-bye to its antiquated electric system and generates power centrally. Water systems improve on still another isle. Everyone is ready to roll on trap day. An island fire department gets a new fire engine. Or a first fire engine. Lobsters, more numerous, bring a good season. An offshore lad gets his own boat and begins to fish out here, staying away from the mainland. A band of minstrels comes ashore and sings chanties for an evening at an island hotel, voices drifting out over the harbor.

Small signs, perhaps, but the stuff of glad hearts and survival. A reprieve in various forms, however modest, for the island community. Once, in a room with poet Robert Frost, I listened to hear him call poetry "a momentary stay against confusion." Islands are such, too. They remind that the best places are not brightly lit. That sleep comes easiest with the sound of waves, wind, and current. That simplicity has its virtues, and that life must have some texture if it is to be worth living. On islands, notions of this sort are as recent as today.

Enjoying Maine's Islands

ISLAND TRAVEL

A grand side benefit of visiting Maine's offshore islands is that you get to make a saltwater voyage, sometimes short, sometimes long, but always immensely pleasing to the eye. Or a spellbinding flight over Maine's legendary coast, with views for dozens of miles up and down the Atlantic shelf. In fact, an interest in island-hopping, quite apart from the islands themselves, justifies the travel described here if only to examine how each isle is situated in Maine's dramatic seas. No substitute exists for the actual going, the sense of change and distance tangible on the salt air, the mainland slipping away along the western horizon until it becomes a mere figment of the traveler's rememberings. This manner of voyaging is in short supply in everyday life and becomes itself a rationale for stealing away to the isles.

The destinations noted in this book can all be reached by scheduled boat service, and several are conveniently visited by air if you have limited free time. Transportation is described at the end of each island chapter in this book. In its earliest years, island transport proved a sometime thing, local operators coming and going, ships drafted into military service, and financial problems dogging the various companies formed to provide haulage. Today the **Maine State Ferry Service**, a government agency, and the **Casco Bay Islands Transit District** provide transport to many of the offshore islands and the chain of islands in inner Casco Bay. Additionally, private operators and tour boats will take you to some smaller islands, such as the Cranberry Isles, in summer. Air service from Owls Head to Matinicus, Vinalhaven, North Haven, and other islands supplements surface transport year-round. On-call air service is available from Owls Head on most days, weather permitting. Air- and water-taxi service are available to various islands from points along the coast. In short, you *can* get there from here.

Still, *regularly scheduled* may need some clarification in Maine. Matinicus has ferry service on that regimen, but *regular* means once every month except for a few weeks in midsummer, when service becomes every few days. Sort of. Where islanders use their own boats to come to the mainland, the frequency of ferry service has declined. (Some would say the order of necessity should be reversed.)

As noted, Matinicus gets by with haulage once a month outside of summer but enjoys daily passenger mail-plane service as compensation. Monhegan has thrice-daily boat service in summer, dwindling to twice-daily trips in the shoulder seasons, and three-times-a-week service during winter. Other islands, such as North Haven or Vinalhaven, have multiple ferry service daily, which dwindles slightly to less frequent service in winter. The larger islands of Casco Bay have frequent daily service the year round. Additional Casco Bay cruise services are added in summer. Schedules and routes described in this book are current at the time of publication but may change without notice. Several islands have regular or "on-call" air service, and the additional expense of flying may be worth its cost when your time is limited or you wish to travel in a narrow window of favorable weather. Fog may prevent flights to various islands for days on end.

When you travel, always confirm schedules with local agencies first.

As you plan your trips to the islands described in this volume, it will be useful to become familiar with the boat or air service provided and to schedule your island visit carefully. In most cases, unless you will be staying overnight, it is wise to take an early boat, giving you a full day on the island before making the return trip in late afternoon. Travelers should be aware that the ferries on some runs also carry cargo and vehicles, and stops may be made to load or unload. Ferries depart promptly, so don't be late. Board early and, if the weather is fair, take an outside seat on the upper decks to enjoy the splendid views as you sail outward.

Unless you absolutely have to take a car to an island, it makes sense to leave it ashore and walk or cycle around the isle you are visiting. In high summer, people ferrying their cars to the islands or back to the mainland can create long lines, and you may have to wait for several ferry departures before getting a vehicle aboard. The only islands described in this volume where a car might be essential are Swans and Islesboro. (The ferry lands several miles from Minturn Village on Swans, and to see the northern limits of Islesboro, a bicycle or car is necessary.) On most other islands, the ferry docks close to the village center, so that you arrive at the hub of island activity and can walk or cycle outward. In any case, why seek the tranquility of an offshore island only to take an automobile there? Should you decide of necessity to ferry a vehicle to any island, be sure to request a *return* reservation at a specific hour to hold space for the trip to the mainland. In high summer, return reservations for vehicles often sell out early.

Air service to many Penobscot Bay island destinations is provided by **Penobscot Island Air (PIA)** from Knox County Regional Airport at Owls Head. The airport is located off ME 73, four miles south of Rockland center. Regularly scheduled service to Matinicus, North Haven, and Vinalhaven flies daily, and to Swans, Criehaven, Stonington, Blue Hill, Islesboro, and other coastal communities and islands on call. PIA flies three aircraft year-round and adds a fourth in summer, plus a Bell 47 helicopter, which is available for direct flights or island tours. The airline also offers water-taxi service in the event that

Touching down at "Matinicus International Airport"

ocean fog restricts flying, and provides van service for local, within-Maine transfers.

Mail flights to Matinicus, North Haven, and Vinalhaven at 8:30 A.M. and 1:00 P.M. offer slightly lower fares, and flight discount ticket books are available for those who would fly to several island destinations, providing about a 30 percent discount. For visitors who arrive on the Maine coast at odd hours and wish to get quickly to the islands rather than waiting for the next day's ferry, air service is available twenty-four hours per day by arrangement. PIA also provides FedEx and UPS package freight connections from several islands. Call Penobscot Island Air Service at (207) 596-7500.

Enjoying Maine's Islands

CLOTHING AND FOOTWEAR

Visitors to Maine's coastal islands should observe the "travel light" maxim. For day trips, a light, waterproof anorak, sweater, sunglasses, binoculars, camera, lunch, and water belong in a day pack. Ferry crossings traverse cold water, and island temperatures are typically cooler than those on the mainland. Visitors staying overnight at island guest houses or inns should add to the above a couple of changes of informal clothing, a rain shell, extra socks, and maybe a hat. Even in high summer it is always wise to expect cool weather, particularly at night. Persons evincing exceptional bravery might pack a bathing suit as well.

Since walking is a staple of island exploration, stout walking shoes or light boots are appropriate footwear. Forget fashion. Island roads may be paved or gravel. Nature preserves, woodlands, parks, shoreline, and rock ledge are rough, and wearing sturdy footgear is necessary.

If you're staying over, take along a couple of those books you've been meaning to read. Quiet island evenings are perfect for reading.

Enjoying Maine's Islands

VISITING RESPECTFULLY

Whenever you visit an offshore island, it is wise to remember that most island terrain is private property. Trails, paths, and even some island roads may cross someone's land. Most islanders are pretty tolerant of such things and don't mind visitors crossing land, but it never hurts to ask. Several islands described in these pages have local parklands and sometimes nature preserves of some size. Please use these lands carefully and inquire as to local regulations. Camping is allowed on some islands, but permission must first be obtained from local authorities. Reservations are required by the National Park Service for camping on Isle au Haut. Open fires are prohibited on most islands.

Most people prefer to travel to the islands and walk the island landscape quietly. If children travel with you, they should always be supervised. Ocean travel and island walks also require that parents keep a sharp watch for children's safety. On ferries, on tour ships, and on islands themselves, children should always be closely monitored for safety's sake. Shoreline or woodland terrain can be wet and very slippery. Cliffs and ledges can prove hazardous.

Sea Queen (beside ramp of second wharf) serves the Cranberry Isles

Islanders often bring dogs on crossings, but always on a leash. It's a good idea not to bring pets to the islands, but if you must, be sure to monitor your dog on the boat and on the island and keep pets tethered.

The Isles of Shoals

Maine's southernmost sea islands lie within that cluster of rocks, ledges, mounds, and bars known as the Isles of Shoals at the mouth of the Piscataqua River, off Newcastle and Kittery. Shared with New Hampshire, the Isles comprise Duck, Appledore, Smuttynose, Cedar, Malaga, Star, Lunging (Londoner), Seavey, and White Islands, the initial five lying within Maine waters, the others belonging to New Hampshire. An article in the July 1898 issue of *New England Magazine* avowed that "Wherever you walk or drive on the sea-coast within several miles of the mouth of the Piscataqua, you are confronted, with more or less distinctness and from the most unexpected points of view, by the Isles of Shoals. In clear weather no vessel can skirt the coast without sighting them, and they cannot have failed to attract the attention of all early navigators in the vicinity." Indeed, for navigators and all those who work the sea, the Shoals have long been the lodestones of Maine's southern coast.

The islands in this group rise on a staggered southwest–northeast line several miles out from Whaleback Light. The southernmost of the chain, New Hampshire's White Island, supports highly visible White Island Light. The three central islands in the group, Smuttynose, Cedar, and Star, are connected by a breakwater that forms the ocean side of Gosport Harbor. Historically, the Isles were a place where ships grounded, ran headlong into ledge in fog, and picked their way gingerly northwest in conflicting tides and currents toward the Piscataqua and the port of Portsmouth. Today massive LNG ships and oil tankers, radar and GPS on full, cautiously find their way past the Isles and up the Piscataqua.

Nathaniel Hawthorne came to the Isles in 1852 and, in his *American Note Books*, said of them: "It is quite impossible to give an idea of these rocky shores—how confusedly they are tossed together, what solid ledges, what great fragments thrown out

A schooner circles White Island Light

PHOTO BY PETER RANDALL

Duck

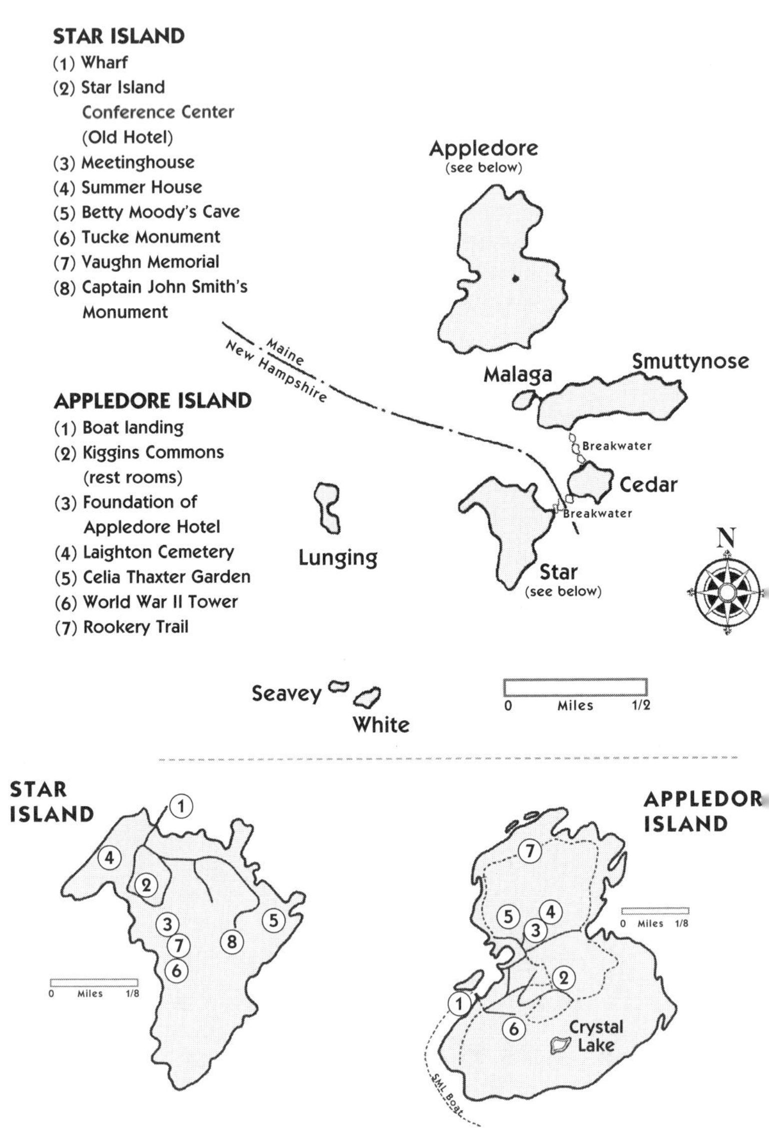
Isles of Shoals
STAR ISLAND
(1) Wharf
(2) Star Island Conference Center (Old Hotel)
(3) Meetinghouse
(4) Summer House
(5) Betty Moody's Cave
(6) Tucke Monument
(7) Vaughn Memorial
(8) Captain John Smith's Monument
APPLEDORE ISLAND
(1) Boat landing
(2) Kiggins Commons (rest rooms)
(3) Foundation of Appledore Hotel
(4) Laighton Cemetery
(5) Celia Thaxter Garden
(6) World War II Tower
(7) Rookery Trail
Appledore
(see below)
Maine
New Hampshire
Malaga
Smuttynose
Breakwater
Cedar
Breakwater
Lunging
Star
(see below)
N
Seavey
White
0 Miles 1/2
STAR ISLAND
0 Miles 1/8
APPLEDOR
ISLAND
0 Miles 1/8
Crystal Lake
SML Boat

from the rest.... It seems as if some of the massive materials of the world remained superfluous, after the Creator had finished, and were carelessly thrown down here, where the millionth part of them emerge from the sea." In the matter of geology, little has changed.

Visitors to the Shoals who come via the Piscataqua will pass Whaleback Light at the mouth of the river. The first lighthouse built here was erected in 1829, a twenty-two-foot-high stone platform with a low tower. This structure soon saw its foundation erode, and the tower itself leaked and flooded in severe weather. The tower was sheathed in metal and the foundation augmented, but lighthouse duty here was anything but secure. In 1869, a second, seventy-five-foot tower of granite was constructed and the old tower was modified to contain a foghorn apparatus. The lighthouse keeper, Captain Leander White, of nearby Newcastle, nearly lost his life when the tower was flooded in an 1886 storm, and the foundation of the old tower was badly damaged in the March snowstorm of 1888. Today the automated beacon still operates, warning ships off the ledges.

Across the river mouth from Gerrish Island stands Newcastle Light, erected as no more than a lantern on a flag mast at Fort William and Mary here in 1774. A more typical lighthouse structure came into service by 1784 under the supervision of Captain Titus Salter. The early light was fed, under contract, with either hake oil or whale oil. A new eighty-foot tower was built in 1804. A fire at the light in 1826 did significant damage to both tower and rescuers. In 1872, a new keeper's house came to be, and in 1877 a fifty-two-foot tower of steel was put in place to support the light.

From the mouth of the Piscataqua, the Shoals arise immediately into view. Settlement at the Isles came very early, the overseas fishing fleets of European nations coming ashore here much as they did on Monhegan far to the north in the 1600s. The Isles as a major fishing station offered shoals of baitfish in shallow waters, anchorage in the lee of the islands, and a shorter trip to the banks offshore where most fishing went on. Sir Christopher Leavitt navigated to land here in 1623 and found the Isles quite desolate, pronouncing, "Upon these I neither could see one good timber tree, nor so much ground as to make a garden." The tiny harbor at Gosport limited its utility as a base, and Leavitt wrote, "The place is found to be a good fishing place for six shippes. . . . The harbor is but indifferent good." A hundred years later, a French ship's log recorded that sixty fishing shallops sailed from the Isles' harbor with roughly 280 men to crew them.

The isles were a monkish place originally. Livestock and women were forbidden here, the first settlers believing, perhaps, that an arduous life would go more successfully if family feuds, romantic alliances, and territorial disputes were avoided. There were at least two taverns on the Isles by 1628, and the place had begun to earn an unsavory reputation.

The female prohibition changed in 1647 when a Portsmouth man, John Reynolds, brought his wife and livestock to the islands and was promptly summoned to the assizes. No less august a body than the Massachusetts General Court ultimately heard the case, and it allowed the woman to remain if she behaved herself, but would not tolerate the pigs and goats the man had imported. The Isles were already barren enough; the presence of multiplying, grazing animals would strip the soil bare, thought the court.

In the 1700s, before the Revolution, the population of the Isles increased to as many as six hundred souls. The cluster of ledges organized itself into a village with a system of local governance, and, of course, those who lived here were bound together by mutual dependence in the dangerous occupation they shared. A school was conducted on the islands and, in the early 1700s, many thought island children better educated than those on the mainland. The Reverend John Tucke ministered to a congregation here for forty years in a chapel built in part from the timbers of a Spanish wreck. Tucke's long tenure had a civilizing effect on the Isles' rough-and-tumble element. The lad who became Sir William Pepperell was born near Appledore at Kittery, Maine, in 1696, his father an Appledore man out of Cornwall in England. Pepperell the younger was a major figure in the Louisbourg campaign of 1745, when New Englanders captured that French fortress on Cape Breton, Nova Scotia. In recognition of that achievement, Pepperell was knighted by

George II in 1746, the first North American colonist to be thus honored.

After the Revolution, the tenor of island life deteriorated. The fishing continued, but many families had been scattered by the war, and these islands became less a community of hard work and reverence than an outpost better known for consumption of West Indian rum. Some captains alleged that the riffraff of the Shoals were putting out lanterns at night to lure ships onto the rocks so that they could be looted. Portsmouth citizens gossiped about the collapse of morality on the islands. One Portsmouth clergyman inveighed: ". . . the condition of poverty and deprivation into which those who remained had lapsed became a matter of public scandal. . . . the Shoalsmen had burned their meetinghouse to the ground. Then, for want of a guiding hand, the always loosely bound society had fallen into the worst depths of immorality." It would be the 1830s before the Isles would regain a sense of respectability. Occasionally disaster struck, too, in the form of shipwreck, mayhem, and disappearance.

The Shoals have long been thought to harbor the ghosts of those pirates who molested ships along the coast and across the northern Atlantic. Old Philip Babb, a constable who resided on the Shoals in the late 1600s, is said to rest uneasy on the Isles, his ghost patrolling about, brandishing his dagger still. Tales of buried treasure are a part of island lore. Captain Quelch is believed to have been caught in the act of hiding treasure here by a troop of Mass-

PHOTO BY PETER RANDALL

Star (foreground), Cedar, Smuttynose, Malaga, and Appledore from above

achusetts militia. Stories claim that the notorious Captain Teach left his wife on the Isles, and her ghost guards his treasure, awaiting his return. Several modern sightings of this bereaved female, her long-tressed apparition wandering about, mouthing mournful pleas for her captain's return, have been reported by astonished visitors.

Travelers to either Appledore or Star will have fine views over to White Island Light, first erected there in 1820. Thomas Laighton of Portsmouth became keeper there in 1839, before embarking on a career as hotelman. Young Benjamin Whaling manned the light as his assistant. The lighthouse saw rebuilding in 1865. On the trip to or from the islands, there are moments when the traveler can see White Island Light, Whaleback Light, and New-castle Light all at once, a rare pleasure.

In 1847, Laighton gave up his keeper's post to assume control of a hotel he'd built on Appledore, and thus began the tradition of island vacationing among New England's well connected. President Franklin Pierce, a New Hampshireman, came here. Literary lights James Russell Lowell, Sarah Orne Jewett, Nathaniel Hawthorne, Harriet Beecher Stowe, John Greenleaf Whittier, and William Dean Howells visited, as did artists such as Childe Has-sam and William Morris Hunt. Laighton's daughter, Celia Laighton Thaxter, became the host of many sa-lons on the island and wrote about her experiences in *Among the Isles of Shoals* and *An Island Garden.* Appledore and, later, Star Islands were not merely for loafing. The intellectual and creative atmosphere fostered here was striking and productive despite the stony isolation, as Thaxter's record of life on the Isles shows. It was a stimulating flowering in an un-likely place.

"Swept by every wind that blows," recorded Thaxter, "and beaten by the brine for unknown ages, well may the Isles of Shoals be barren, bleak and bare. At first sight nothing can be more rough and inhospitable than they appear. . . . Landing for the first time, the stranger is struck only by the sadness of the place, the vast loneliness;—for there are not even trees to whisper with familiar voices,—nothing but sky and sea and rocks. But the very wildness and desolation reveal a strange beauty to him." It was for this sere beauty and the quiet that guests came, often year after year. Many still do.

Thaxter's sometime guest Nathaniel Hawthorne wrote of the barren isles after a first visit: "It is quite impossible to give an idea of these rocky shores—how confusedly they are bound together, lying in all directions: what solid ledges, what great frag-

PHOTO BY PETER RANDALL

Celia Thaxter's garden on Appledore has been carefully restored.

ments thrown out from the rest . . . in the course of thousands of years have become partially bestrewn with a little soil."

Today the Shoals are centers of investigation and research at the Shoals Marine Laboratory, on Appledore. The University of New Hampshire and Cornell University have jointly operated marine and avian research programs here. The islands are uniquely located for studying marine birds, other migrating species, and marine organisms. An incautious walk in certain island spots will bring flocks of diving birds, angrily protecting their nests. The Unitarian-Universalist Association, which owns Star Island, has held residential conferences each summer since 1897 in what was once the old Oceanic Hotel.

As mentioned before, visitors to the Isles will in-

Gosport, Star Island. Stone is the building material of choice on the Shoals.

PHOTO BY PETER RANDALL

evitably hear stories of how these islands slipped into debauchery periodically, including police raids on the entangled community that grew through intermarriage, cohabitation, and casual alliance. Add sufficient quantities of Barbados rum and the presence of passing sailors to that mix, and you have the horrified response from shore dwellers noted earlier. And then there is the small matter of murder.

On a cold night in March 1873, one Louis Wagner turned a stolen dory out of Portsmouth Harbor after dark and rowed hard for Smuttynose. Wagner had observed that most of the men from the fishing families were ashore picking up bait and supplies and, perhaps, having an evening of drink. He thus expected to find Karen and Anetha Christensen, sisters-in-law, and little Maren Christensen alone in their isolated house. Wagner was possessed with

the notion that money and treasure were hidden in their premises, and that they could be his simply for the taking.

Wagner rode the current downriver and then rowed steadily southeast toward the Isles. Quietly pulling his boat up on Smuttynose, his way lit only by the fading moon, he proceeded to the lonely house. One can scarce imagine the awful mayhem the madman created there, murdering the two screaming older women with an ax while young Maren fled in her nightclothes over the blooded snow. She secreted herself with her dog, shivering through the night in hiding, until able to signal others on Appledore at dawn. Wagner got little for his adventure that night except some strenuous rowing and an eventual hanging. He was arrested, convicted, and two years later swung from a gallows at Maine's Thomaston Penitentiary, one of the last souls so accommodated in the state of Maine, which decided it didn't like hanging after all in 1879.

Other tragedies have had their day on these rocks. The Captain Samuel Haley family was prominent on Smuttynose in the early 1800s and awoke one morning in January 1813 to find fourteen dead and frozen Spanish sailors on the ledges outside their door. During a tempestuous night, the ship *Sagunto* had gone aground in a snowstorm, all hands perishing. It was merely one of many that would come to grief on the Shoals, its crew dashed on the rocks as their ship broke into pieces.

Earlier, in the long series of skirmishes that pitted Indians against British settlers from the 1660s to the 1750s, there were tribal raids on the fishing community at the islands. During an Indian raid in 1724, Betty Moody found herself alone with her child in an isolated house, both ripe for harm. The absence of sheltering woods on the islands left her little place to hide. She fled quickly along the shoreline rocks and found a tiny cave in which to shelter herself and her infant. She covered the child's mouth to prevent it crying out as the raiders walked overhead. The Indians did not find her, but the woman discovered with sorrow that she had accidentally suffocated her child in the attempt to quiet it. Walkers here today still find Betty Moody's cave and, perhaps, her ghost as well.

Along the shore of Star Island rests Miss Underhill's Chair. For years, Nancy Underhill was the schoolteacher in the little village center of Gosport. The schoolmistress had discovered a chairlike spot on the coastal rocks where she preferred to sit and watch the sea at the end of the day. In 1852, while enjoying the view, the teacher was swept away by a great rush of water that rose and scoured the ledges. She was later found, drifted ashore and quite dead, well north at York, her lessons at last finished.

Ownership of the Isles now lies in private or government hands. Day-trippers usually visit only Star Island, site of the Unitarian-Universalists' Star Island Corporation Conference Center, where a series of weeklong religious conferences progresses

PHOTO BY PETER RANDALL

Islanders of another era sleep on Appledore.

throughout the summer. The fine old clapboard hotel is still here, part of the conference center. The distinctive steeple of the stone meetinghouse rises above the barren landscape, and lantern-lit services are held in the building on summer evenings. Before the lighthouse on White Island was constructed, parishioners placed lanterns in the church steeple as a warning to approaching ships.

Paths roam the island, and wildflowers choke these paths, growing profusely and brilliantly in the bright, moist air. Strollers find pastures of blossoms that dip to coastal coves. Visitors may also tour the university marine research facilities by permission and prior arrangement. The laboratory's workboat ferries visitors from Star to Appledore on request during summer daytime hours.

For those who land at the Isles, a walk around Star will take in the island's summer conference center, Betty Moody's Cave, and a monument to the aforementioned Reverend Tucke. The Vaughan family and the variously present Captain John Smith have memorials here, too. Those who go over to Appledore will find the premises of the Shoals Marine Laboratory (with restroom facilities at Kiggins Commons), the plot in which members of the Laighton family were buried, and Celia Thaxter's famous garden. (Garden admission fees help fund scholarships for Shoals Marine Laboratory undergrads.) If you come ashore, inquire on the islands for directions to these local landmarks, most of which are easy to find, given the lack of forest cover.

Some would argue that these islands belong first and foremost to the droves of seabirds that nest here. Arthur Borror, the University of New Hampshire's associate director of the Shoals Marine Laboratory, estimates that nearly six thousand birds nest locally, mainly herring gulls and great black-backed gulls. More than two hundred species of birds have been tagged on the islands, including many migrators. People who stroll near the major nesting sites jaunt about holding a stick in the air over their heads, as if preparing for Guy Fawkes

Day. This seems to deter the diving wild birds that are intolerant of humans near their nests in early summer.

Duck Island, north of Appledore, barely rises above the tide and gets the wash of high waves. Still, some eleven hundred pairs of double-crested cormorants nest on Duck, and ducks and seals use the island, too.

Despite their seemingly barren, inhospitable character, the nine Isles of Shoals are a grand, natural point of intersection around which wildlife, the wind, and the sea arrange themselves, as some would have it, for eternity.

GETTING THERE

The **Isles of Shoals Steamship Company (ISSCO)** provides regular nine-island tour service in season from its 315 Market Street wharf in Portsmouth, New Hampshire. At the time this book went to press, ISSCO had decided not to offer its usual twice-per-day round trips landing at the Isles of Shoals in 2005. The company's tours *around* the isles and trips up the Piscataqua River to Great Bay will continue to be offered. The ticket office is on Market Street just off I-95 via the last New Hampshire exit (Exit 7) before crossing the high-level bridge into Maine. From I-95, follow Market Street eastward until you see signs. Call (603) 431-5500 or (800) 441-4620 for sailing schedules. Their Web site is: www.islesofshoals.com.

Portsmouth Harbor Cruises aboard the *Heritage* will also tour *around* (but not land at) the Shoals in summer. Their base is located on Ceres Street on the Portsmouth waterfront next to the tugboats. Parking is available at the nearby municipal garage on "the hill." Contact Portsmouth Harbor Cruises at (800) 776-0915 or (603) 436-8084. Visit their Web site at www.portsmouthharborcruises.com.

Sail *Amaryllis* also offers sailing journeys *around* the Isles from Portsmouth on a forty-five-foot catamaran. Cruises that anchor offshore of the Shoals overnight are available. Contact: (603) 205-0630 or visit their Web site at: www.sailamaryllis.com.

Local trips to the isles that offer day-trippers an opportunity to land and walk about are provided by **Island Cruises**. Their boat, *Uncle Oscar,* leaves from the Town Dock, off Route 1A in Rye, New Hampshire, next door to Portsmouth. Connect with them at (603) 964-6446 or www.uncleoscar.com. Also ferrying day-trippers to the isles is ***The Prince of Whales***, out of Newburyport, Massachusetts. Their Monday cruises land on Star Island. Try www.welikewhales.com or (800) 848-1111.

At the time of publication, Star Island Corporation was arranging boat service to the Isles and conference center for 2005, though it was unclear whether the private Star Island service would also offer public transport to day travelers. See their Web site for updates: www.starisland.org.

A day around or on the Isles requires a trip out in early morning from Portsmouth or Rye, New Hampshire, or Newburyport, Massachusetts, allowing plenty of time for walking along island paths and picnicking on the rocks if you choose to go ashore. A visit to the Shoals Marine Laboratory makes an interesting introduction to current marine research.

ACCOMMODATIONS AND MEALS

Visitors are advised to bring their own food and water with them. The conference center on Star Island operates a snack bar that has, in past years, been open to use by day visitors.

There are no overnight accommodations on the Isles for casual travelers. Please respect the fragile environment of these islands and carry out your trash as you return to the mainland.

Casco Bay Isles

Casco Bay is a vast pool of islands, sounds, scattered lighthouses, oceangoing ship traffic, fishing activity, and kayakers out for a stroll. Close to Portland yet distinctly apart, the numerous islands of Casco Bay are of all sizes and inclinations, and a welcome respite from Maine's busiest region onshore. The bay reminds one of how quickly, in Maine, one can step from settled prem-

Looking down channel, Cliff Island

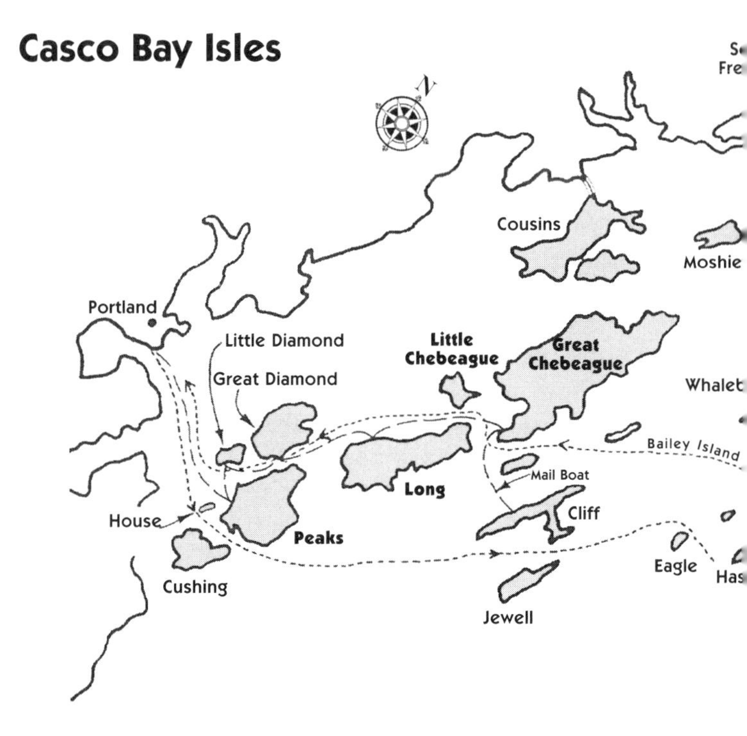

ises to the saltwater world—a world, too, of hospitable islands.

Inner Casco Bay boasts a chain of islands, some of which make excellent destinations for day trips or overnight journeys. There are Great and Little Chebeague, Long, Peaks, Great and Little Diamond, Cousins, Cliff, and several hundred others with names like Lower Goose, Little Whaleboat, and Ministerial. This expansive collection has been long referred to as the Calendar Isles, based on the assumption that within the wide limits of Casco Bay there are 365 islands, one for every day of the year.

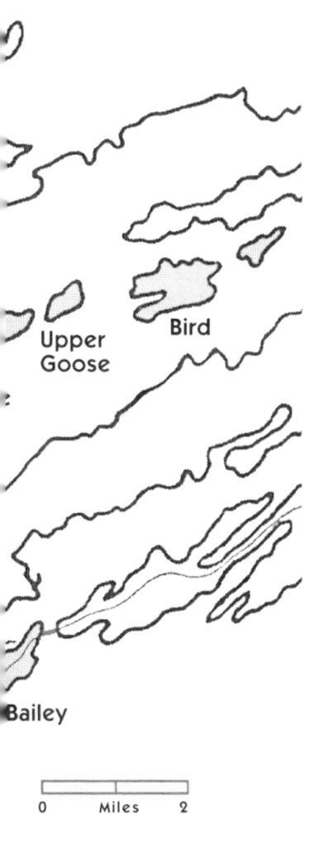

Many are privately held, locations of small cottage colonies or isolated residences. Many more are mere ledges, awash with the changing tide, their only regular visitors herring gulls and wind. Sounds shape the flow of current here as well: Luckse, Broad, Merriconeag, Hussey are highways of water.

Here, we introduce travelers to three settled islands of Inner Casco Bay: Long Island, with its wonderful quiet, outstanding seaward sand beach and round-island roads for walking; Great Chebeague, largest island of the group, with good walking, bicycling, and accommodations; and Peaks Island, an interesting place, with fine ocean-side roads, restaurants for a meal or a pint on your way home, and accommodations for those who would stay over.

Great and Little Diamond and Cliff islands also enjoy regular ferry service, but we will skip those three, as they are largely private small communities and, with exception of the dockside restaurant at Diamond Pass, are not really set up for day visitors.

An excellent introduction to Casco Bay's islands is provided by Casco Bay Lines' Bailey Island Tour Service, which sets out from Portland, skirts the

Looking forward to an island jaunt in Casco Bay

major islands described here, comes ashore at Mackerel Cove on Bailey Island, with a pause for lunch, and then returns through the midst of the islands described in this section. Once you've got the lay of the land, you'll find the means to visiting Long, Great Chebeague, and Peaks on the pages that follow.

Casco Bay Isles

LONG ISLAND

Long Island sequesters itself well up Casco Bay, but in sight of Portland, Maine's largest city. Roughly six miles up the channel, Long may seem close to the city if you gaze toward the southern horizon, but, in feeling, the island carries on in a separate world. Visited before 1600, Long Island was slow to settle, passed through a number of hands, and did not become an active island community until the middle 1700s. The mail boat from Portland stops here a couple of times a day, and one or two other ferries on a regular passenger schedule, but Long keeps to itself otherwise, a quiet, independent place.

Long Island carried its sense of independence further a few years back when its residents, tired of paying property taxes to the city of Portland and getting very little in return, petitioned the Maine legislature to sever its ties with the larger city and became a separate community. It looked as though some other Casco Bay islands might follow suit, and suddenly Portland began paying attention to its island communities, eager to prevent them from following Long's example. Long Islanders seem pleased with their secession, and now use their taxes to benefit the island rather than paving streets in distant, mainland Portland.

Herbert Jones, onetime Portland author and bookseller, called Long the "Isle of Clambakes and Chowders." Jones was referring to the gigantic picnics and clambakes held on the island's shores, as people arrived by boat in a celebratory mood from all over. Here were served fish chowders of singular repute, concocted to recipes submitted by Maine notables. Such feasts were common around the bay in the Victorian era. Thousands dug in for Portland's 1886 Centennial fest, when sixteen cords of wood were used to roast five hundred bushels of clams. In that era, Long also boasted three fine hotels noted for their cooking. The last of these emporiums, the Granite Springs Hotel, was torn down in 1913.

South of Chebeague and northeast of Great Diamond, Long Island was first named by Dutch visitors, and first actively claimed by Sir Ferdinando Gorges of London as part of a much larger royal grant in the region. Long consists of roughly a thousand acres, its narrow, slender shape running north and south, its eastern periphery fronting the open Atlantic. At the island's southern end lies Harbor de Grace, an indentation named by Bordeaux sailor Louis Elerette, which, historically, has offered protected, ice-free anchorage. "Singing" or Andrews Beach is close by, a sand-and-pebble crescent whose variegated surface seems to produce a sort

Long Island

(1) General store
(2) VFW Hall
(3) Tennis court
(4) Church, gift shop, library

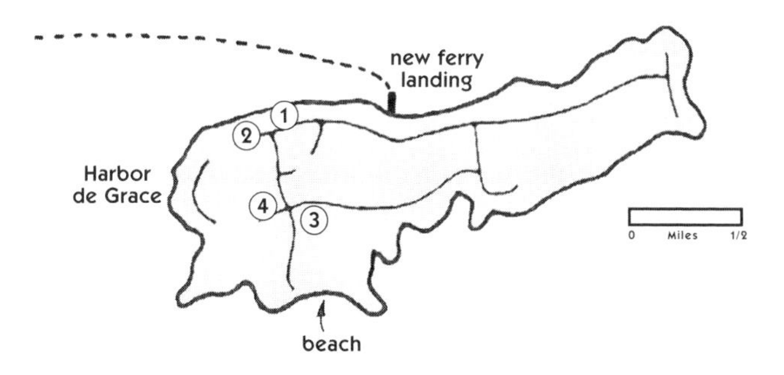

of whistling sound when wind and tide are right. The island is served by several roads that will carry you its length and breadth from the new wharf where ferryboats land with passengers, mail, and cargo. On Long's ocean side a superb sand beach lies hidden, its arc sheltered by Junk o' Pork and other ledges and bars to seaward. (See the author's *Walking the Maine Coast* for information on walks here.)

Indians used Long as a base for fishing, camping on its sheltered western shore and enjoying water from the island's numerous springs. Long apparently owes its early settlement to the Sears family of Boston, John Sears arriving here in 1640. Captain George Luxton probably brought his family to the island at about this time as well. Richard Russell and, later, his son James owned Long from 1667 and later sold it to John Smith in 1706. The Searses, Luxtons, Russells, and Smiths—plus one or two other families—left their imprint on the island more or less alone until driven off in sporadic Indian hostilities.

It would be the proprietor of nearby Cushing Island who would spur settlement on Long after 1700. Ezekiel Cushing got his hands on Long through what was certainly an error of judgment, bartering a choice piece of in-town Portland real estate for the remote isle. Cushing nevertheless made money out of his purchase as others migrated to the island and purchased lots for farmsteads and dockage. By 1830, a number of families totaling nearly 150 souls had established themselves on Long. Settling in comfortably, Cushing is said to have lived the life of a grandee on his island, being driven about Long in a fine black chaise by his servant Cato and pulled by a matched pair of bays.

The island's later settlers were nearly all fishermen to a man, and farming also became common as land was cleared. The combined occupations made it possible to live a modest but self-sufficient life. During Prohibition, Long Island is said to have transshipped more than its share of Canadian whiskey with few the wiser, confirming the notion that fishing craft might be used for other purposes handily in the name of opportunity. (Of course, such stories cannot possibly be true.) Long today is an island community occupied year-round, some of its residents engaged in traditional occupations, others

Waiting for the ferry

retired, with many arriving as summer tenants or visitors. And then there are those residents of Portland proper who know that the ocean side of Long offers a beautiful, uncrowded escape from the city on a hot summer day, and who come to the island accordingly.

Long is easily reached via Casco Bay Lines ferries, and a morning outward departure is advisable. Ferries visit Long somewhat less frequently than other islands closer to the city. In winter, schedules constrict further, so a day excursion goes best if you arrive on an early boat and plan to head back to the mainland by mid- to late afternoon. Those who love to walk or bicycle will find Long a perfect destination. You can walk or cycle to the beach, to the

A Casco Bay Lines ferry

island's northern limits, or make a complete circuit of the wooded island at a leisurely pace.

The passage to Long Island is a pretty one, and travelers will see stately Portland Head Light far to the southeast as they move through Portland Harbor before turning north up the channel between rows of other isles. The light was constructed originally in 1787 to a height of fifty-eight feet at the behest of George Washington. Treasury Secretary Alexander Hamilton authorized an increase in the tower's elevation so it could be more easily seen from the southeast. Captain Joseph Greenleaf became the light's first keeper, appointed by President Washington in January 1791. A new, brighter Fresnel lens was installed in 1855. The light was still not seen as bright enough by some. The tower's height got a further increase of another eight feet and an improved, higher-order lens installed a decade later. In 1877, a twenty-four-inch caloric engine that drove a horn from Boston Light was installed, replacing a foghorn carried earlier to the light from Monhegan. In 1885, the light saw reclassification as a second-order station with an accompanying widening of the upper tower and a further lens replacement. Henry Wadsworth Longfellow, born in Portland, had visited the important light and remembered it thus:

> And as the evening darkens,
> lo! how bright
> Through the deep purple of the
> twilight air,
> Beams forth the sudden radiance
> of its light
> With strange unearthly splendour
> in its glare!

ACCOMMODATIONS AND MEALS

Those wishing to spend a night on quiet Long Island will find rooms at the **Chestnut Hill Bed and**

Breakfast, Beach Avenue, Long Island, ME 04050, tel. (207) 766-5272. The **Spar Restaurant** on Island Avenue is open seasonally, tel. (207) 766-3310.

GETTING THERE

At the foot of the Franklin Street Arterial at Commercial Street in Portland, **Casco Bay Lines** (the Casco Bay Islands Transit District) runs frequent daily ferry service from the Portland Ferry Terminal to Long Island. A **mail-boat run** stops at Long twice daily. On a seasonal schedule, the extended **island tour** also leaves the Portland terminal for Bailey Island, passing near Long on its way. Sailing times for all services change quarterly. Call (207) 774-7871 for information.

Portland can be reached several times daily by interstate bus service (Greyhound, Vermont Transit, and Concord Trailways) and four times daily via Amtrak's Downeaster rail service from and to Boston. The Portland International Jetport (PWM) is served by several national airlines from most major U.S. cities. The ferry terminal is a short taxi ride from these various services.

Casco Bay Isles

GREAT CHEBEAGUE

For those who will ferry up the length of inner Casco Bay, Great Chebeague, the Abenaki "isle of many springs," awaits. This more than 2000-acre island is the largest of the Casco Bay archipelago, a place of bays and elevations with a sizable year-round population and such amenities as shops, pleasant inn and bed-and-breakfast accommodations, and, yes, even a small golf course.

The island rests on a long history of Indian and European occupation, white settlement beginning, perhaps, as early as 1743. The Merry family of Boston gained title to the island from Sir Ferdinando Gorges, who held royal letters patent to the area, and soon sold it at a profit to John King. Yarmouth man Walter Gendall acquired the island from King but paid for it with his life, ambushed by Indians. The king's agent, Colonel Thomas Westbrook, once owned the island, too. Westbrook had used his office to make a sizable fortune delivering mast trees, which were cut inland of present-day Portland, to the British navy. A community just west of Portland has taken his name. After passing through the hands of a number of other speculators, the island became the property of several of Boston's religious elders, who promptly named Chebeague "Recompense Island" in accord with their ardent ministries to Natives here.

Early names here are Chandler and Hamilton, Zachariah Chandler purchasing land on Chebeague from the First Church in Boston in 1743. He brought along ten brothers and sisters who also cleared land and settled. Scottish-born Ambrose Hamilton arrived in 1760 as a hundred-acre homesteader. Young Ambrose cleared a farmstead on the island's north shore, married, and set about populating this place, fathering fourteen children and owning to seventy-one grandchildren. Descendants of both families are still on the island today.

Winter snows recede on Chebeague

Great Chebeague

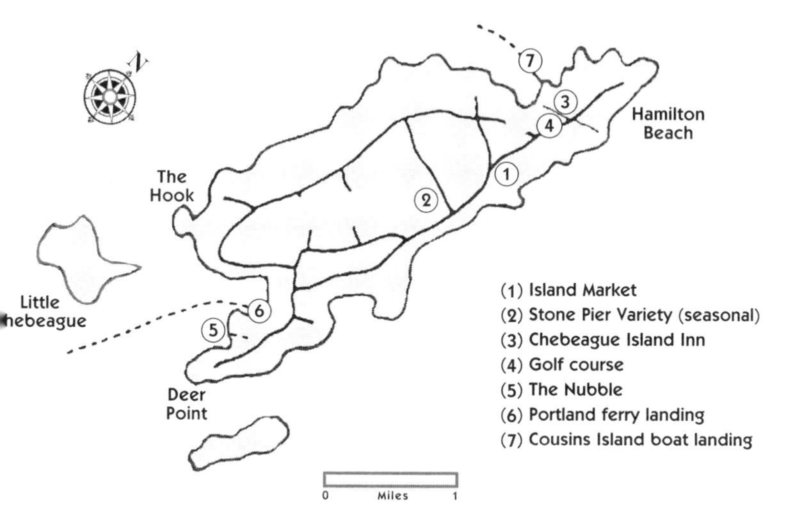

From Chebeague, the Hamilton family mounted a successful coasting business. Chebeague men and boats regularly carried Maine granite quarried to the north to building sites all along the eastern seaboard. Timber on Chebeague became the staple of island boatbuilding, these sloops in turn carrying stone that became part of the Washington Monument, the U.S. Naval Academy at Annapolis, and other prominent structures. Sometimes known as the Hamilton Stone Fleet, the family's flotilla of nearly thirty wooden ships transported Maine stone used in lighthouses, harbor walls, forts, jetties, and breakwaters throughout the mid–nineteenth century. The work courted danger at times. As cargo,

The Chebeague Island Transportation Company's Cousins-to-Chebeague ferry

granite was prone to shifting in tumultuous seas, and periodically stone sloops went down, taking their unfortunate crews with them.

Chebeague's boatbuilding trade got its start through the efforts of Ebenezer Hill, a Cliff Island fellow who married one of the Hamilton women. After the War of 1812, Hill built a home on the island and tried his hand at shipbuilding. Working with merely the simplest of tools and local timber, Hill constructed the *Decatur* and other seaworthy fully-rigged craft. The Seabury, Ricker, Ross, and Bennett families followed Hill in the building and shipfitting trade. Island boatbuilding was and is in the blood of Maine people.

As with many offshore islands, Chebeague was used first by Indians, who left their inland lodges in summer and came to fish, hunt for seals, and, perhaps, take small whales for their oil. *Chebidisco*, they sometimes called this place of pleasant summer living and plentiful food supplies. Remnants of Indian culture have occasionally been found on the island, and several large shell heaps still linger here. Relations between Abenaki peoples and white settlers were said to have been more cordial and tolerant on Chebeague than elsewhere. But even here, the effects of King Philip's War engendered conflict, and the island eventually suffered the same clearances as did others in the region.

Chebeague was a remote place and unchurched until the arrival of a settled minister in 1804. In Chebeague's earliest days of settlement, a North Yarmouth preacher came to the island occasionally

Chebeague's structures come in all shapes and sizes

Looking north over inner Casco Bay from Chebeague's stone pier

by rowboat to attend to souls. Later, the island sometimes saw the presence of the itinerant preacher Abraham Cummings, who was described by Herbert Jones as clad in a voluminous blue cloak that covered him like a tent, giving him more the appearance of a Salem hangman. Preacher Cummings arrived under sail on a doughty catboat from the mainland. His Methodist counterpart was the Reverend Stephen Bennett, who sermonized on Peaks and some of the other islands. Jones has written that Bennett preached so loud and so long that his shouted invocations could be heard with a certain veiled discomfort on neighboring islands. These neighboring communities, it appears, were ever careful not to encourage Mr. Bennett to linger on their turf and to find places of hiding on Sundays when his boat hove into view.

Great Chebeague can be walked or cycled as a

loop, taking the road up the island's east side all the way to Hamilton Beach and then back through the center toward the Hook, at the island's southwest corner. This route also takes the hiker past the island's central district, store, and inn. Chebeague is roughly four and a half miles in length, so walkers or cyclists will get a solid workout here making the full circuit. By paying attention to the tides, it's also possible to walk across the sandbar between Great and Little Chebeague at low tide and to visit the smaller island. Uninhabited Little Chebeague possesses an attractive sand beach for picnicking. It saw various uses by the military in World War II, its past of grand houses having long disappeared by then.

Great Chebeague, because of its distance from the main wharves of Portland, developed more slowly than did other, proximate destinations, such as Peaks Island. Regular transport arrived in the form of the *Charles W. Warren*, which began weekly service to Great Chebeague in 1875. This ship was succeeded by the steamer *Henrietta*, which islanders financed themselves, a venture ending badly for those who invested. The *Alice* and *Gordon* followed, and then the ships of the Harpswell Steamboat Company, the *Sebascodegan*, *Aucocisco*, and *Merryconeag*. Larger ships were needed, both for their carrying capacity and for their ability to break ice in Casco Bay. In the significantly colder winters of the nineteenth century, the bay iced over frequently. Unless vessels could break ice, cargo had to be sledged over the frozen sheet to Chebeague, a not uncommon practice before the advent of more powerful ships.

ACCOMMODATIONS AND MEALS

From late May until mid-October, visitors will find meals and accommodation at the **Chebeague Island Inn** in the island's northeast quarter. The inn's dining room is open to the public. The Chebeague Island Inn, P.O. Box 492, South Road, Gt. Chebeague Island, ME 04017, tel. (800) 569-2288 or (207) 846-5155. Try also the **Chebeague Orchard Inn** at 453 North Road, Gt. Chebeague Island, ME 04017, tel. (207) 846-9488, open year-round. Also open throughout the year is the **Sunset House Bed and Breakfast**, 74 South Road, Gt. Chebeague Island, ME 04017, tel. (207) 846-6568. The Sunset has moorings available to guests who are boaters. The **Island Market** and the **Stone Pier Variety** offer do-it-yourself lunch ingredients and beverages.

GETTING THERE

Today Great Chebeague can be visited by taking the **Casco Bay Lines** ferry from Portland (at the foot of the Franklin Street Arterial at Commercial Street). The **mail boat** offers a view of all the island communities of the inner bay as it makes its way north to Chebeague. The ferryboats tie up on the island's southwest corner.

An extended **island tour** also leaves the Portland terminal for Bailey Island on a seasonal schedule, passing near Chebeague on its way.

Chebeague may also be more directly reached via **Chebeague Island Transportation Company (CTC)** ferry service from Cousins Island. It is necessary to leave your car at the Town of Cumberland satellite parking lot on US 1, and then take the shuttle bus to the wharf on Cousins. The CTC ferry lands on Chebeague's northeast shore at the Stone Pier below the Chebeague Inn.

Sailing times for **Casco Bay Lines** ferry services change quarterly. Call (207) 774-7871.

For the **Chebeague Island Transportation Company,** call (207) 846-3700 or visit their web site at wwwchebeaguetrans.com, where there are directions and schedules.

Portland can be reached several times daily by interstate bus service (Greyhound, Vermont Transit, and Concord Trailways) and four times daily via Amtrak's Downeaster rail service from and to Boston. The Portland International Jetport (PWM) is served by several national airlines from most major U.S. cities. The ferry terminal is a short taxi ride from these various services.

Casco Bay Isles

PEAKS ISLAND

If you stand on Portland's high Eastern Promenade and look seaward, Peaks Island is visible across the broad expanse of Portland Harbor beyond the profiles of House and Little Diamond Islands. Peaks is the most populous of all the isles in two-hundred-square-mile Casco Bay. A twenty-minute ferry ride away, it is a residential isle, part of the

Peaks Island waterfront

social fabric of Portland yet apart and with a chiseled personality of its own. The community on Peaks is eclectic and includes everyone from lobstermen and working people of all sorts to retirees, business types, doctors, and lawyers who commute to the mainland. For many years an inexpensive place to live, Peaks was a quiet neighborhood of small houses and summer cottages where you could purchase a cheap fixer-upper within sight of the water. Today it has been discovered, and even its old coastal gun emplacements have been converted into residences. The older community leavens the new, thankfully. The island has maintained its interesting character, and makes an excellent Casco Bay destination on a brisk winter afternoon or hot summer day.

Peaks boasts 720 acres above the tide line and is home to a year-round population of roughly 1700—a number that more than triples in high summer. Typical of islands in the region, Peaks' bulk runs north and south, its lengthy eastern shore fronting the bold Atlantic. The island supports a network of winding, narrow streets bordered by cottages, modest year-round homes, and a burgeoning number of large, new, expensive palaces.

Peaks has always been a great place for walkers and cyclists. Roads bisect and circle the island, and you can make a day of exploring the island on foot or pedaling along the shore. While a developed center occupies the middle and south end of the island, Peaks' northern lands are less built up, and there are attractive wooded sections along the roads that lead to the island's eastern shore.

This is where Peaks comes into its own. You can walk or cycle here for several miles with splendid ocean views off the ledges and shingle strands that line the shore. In summer, sea breezes cool these spots, making them a welcoming place to picnic while Portland simmers. In the cold months, ocean winds and rolling surf make strolling here invigorating. The island is, in fact, quite as appealing in winter as in the warm months, and a hot grog in a wharfside eatery will warm you up while waiting for the return boat to the mainland.

The island's history is similar to that of others in Casco Bay. Settlement came at the turn of the 1600s, and Peaks is mentioned rhapsodically by English explorer Christopher Leavitt in his journals of 1623. The Bracketts and Palmers were first families, but fled the island to escape Indian raids in 1689. The island had the name of Palmers for some years, and then was variously called Munjoy, Mitton, and Michael's Island, after a number of other prominent island families. Ultimately, Samuel Peaks took the widow Munjoy as his bride, and the island had a new name. Leavitt, who built a house on adjacent House Island, enthused about the pleasant anchorage that Peaks, House, Little Diamond, and Cushing Islands made together: "There are foure islands which make one good harbor, there is very good fishing, much fowle, and the mayne as good ground as any could desire." He became a friend to local Indians, and admired their considerable skills, finding, for example, that their fishing lines were more skillfully made, beautiful, and serviceable than the English equivalent. Leavitt traveled with Indians as they fished and learned from them as he explored the coast around Peaks and nearby inland rivers.

Peaks came into its own with permanent settlement in the late 1700s and assumed its role as Portland's playground in the 1830s. Boardinghouses and cottages took their place here, and Peaks became a kind of recreational garden for the city of Portland and environs. William Jones opened the

Peaks Island

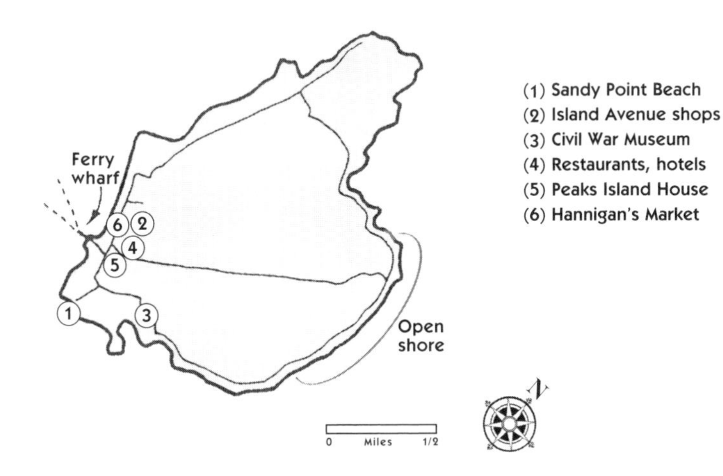

first island hotel in Casco Bay on Peaks in 1850. Jones began luring mainlanders to Peaks by opening an eating place that became known for its seafood. One Portland author has since dubbed Peaks in its heyday the "Isle of Arcady."

In 1869, Peaks was the scene of the tragic wreck of the ship *Helen Eliza*, which plowed into island ledge during a storm and was picked to pieces by the waves. Local legend says that only a single crewman survived. Ominously, he had also been the lone survivor of a shipwreck in the Caribbean. Wishing to avoid testing his luck a third time, the man moved inland, left the seagoing life, and took up farming. There he promptly fell off a log bridge over a river and drowned.

In its heyday, Peaks had something for everyone. In the European manner, guests bowled at the outdoor alleys built on the island, walked the shore, bathed in the island's cold bay waters, and took the island air, which was believed to have certain healing properties. Watercraft parades, roller polo, and waterfront festivals in all seasons drew attention. The Forest City Skating Rink offered visitors a chance to try out their moves, and dancing went on enthusiastically at the Greenwood, a romantic meeting place if you imagined it so. Drama came to Peaks in the form of America's first summer players company in 1887 at the now long-disappeared Pavilion Theatre. The enterprise survived, and Peaks earned a reputation as a favorite summer spot for New York and Boston thespians, famous Broadway names of the era arriving each year to play leading roles within sound of the ocean.

As interest in the island grew, a whole fleet of competing ferry services sprang up on the bay, beginning with the odd-shaped *Antelope* in 1851, which is reported to have looked more like an oversized wheelbarrow than a swift animal. Later, the *Forest City*, the *Greenwood*, *Forest Queen*, and *Emita* plied Casco Bay waters, carrying hundreds and then thousands to the island.

Today a fine outing on Peaks might include turning left at the ferry landing and wending your way north and east along the island roads, with views across to Little Diamond Island. This route will eventually take you out to land's end with views north to other bay islands. The shore road also turns

Southeast Cove on Peaks Island

The cliffs of Cushing Island seen from Peaks

east up a rise and opens up to offer grand views toward Casco Bay's outer islands and the rolling Atlantic. There are very few cars on the island's roads, and you can walk above the water at leisure, selecting a rock promontory on which to have a picnic lunch. The shore road, if followed, continues around Peaks' exposed Atlantic border with good views to islands and bars farther out. The road eventually returns one to the village center while offering some outstanding harbor views. The entire circuit of the island's perimeter consumes a good five miles.

With in-migration, Peaks offers more amenities than most Casco Bay islands. There are several eateries open in summer and at least one in winter, a grocery store, overnight accommodations, an art gallery or two, and bicycle rentals, all located near the ferry landing. At the end of a round-island hike, whatever the season, it is pleasant enough just to sit down somewhere near the wharves and enjoy the view over to Portland, watching the considerable boat traffic come and go.

ACCOMMODATIONS AND MEALS

Peaks, the most populous of the Casco Bay isles, has, at the time of writing, three restaurants, a bakery, two galleries, a grocery market, a general store, and a bike rental shop. The **Peaks Island House** on Island Avenue has rooms for rent, tel. (207) 766-4406. Its restaurant serves meals to the public, tel. (207) 766-4400. Another eatery is **Jones Landing** on Welch Street, tel. (207) 766-5542. Try also the **Peaks Cafe** on Welch Street, tel. (207) 766-2479. **Hannigan's Market** just above the ferry landing makes sandwiches, as does the **Peaks Island Mercantile** on Island Avenue.

For bike rentals, visit **Brad's Recycled Bike Shop** on Island Avenue, calling ahead to reserve a bike at (207) 766-5631. Kayakers will find lessons and rentals at **Maine Island Kayak**, tel. (800) 796-2373 or (207) 766-2373. Public restrooms are available at the **Community Center** building on Island Avenue. There are no formal public picnic grounds, but walkers will find many suitable spots on the sea ledges. Please carry out any trash and respect the privacy of landowners.

GETTING THERE

At the foot of the Franklin Street Arterial at Commercial Street in Portland, **Casco Bay Lines** (the Casco Bay Islands Transit District) runs daily ferry service from the Portland Ferry Terminal to Peaks. Frequent direct service to the island takes about twenty minutes. General information on ferry schedules and conditions to all the islands served by Casco Bay Lines is available at (207) 774-7871. All sailing schedules are subject to change without notice. Call the local ferry offices to confirm current routes, service interruptions, and schedules.

Portland can be reached several times daily by interstate bus service (Greyhound, Vermont Transit, and Concord Trailways) and four times daily via Amtrak's Downeaster rail service from and to Boston. The Portland International Jetport (PWM) is served by several national airlines from most major U.S. cities. The ferry terminal is a short taxi ride from these various services.

Ferry approaching Peaks, House Island in background

Muscongus Bay

MONHEGAN

If you stand slightly to the left of Port Clyde's Marshall Point Light and stare southward, miles beyond the ledges and a chain of smaller islands, a great lump of land rears itself in the company of a smaller mound well to seaward. Those smaller mounds are Thompson, Davis, Benner, Allen, and Burnt Islands. Presuming a clear day when the Nova Scotia Current and the Gulf Stream are not working together to produce some foggy extravaganza, the

Port Clyde Harbor

Monhegan

(1) Ferry landing
(2) Island Inn
(3) Monhegan House
(4) Trailing Yew
(5) Hitchcock House
(6) Fish Beach
(7) Stores (both sides of road)
(8) Lighthouse and museum
(9) Schoolhouse
(10) Tribler Cottage
(11) Cathedral Woods
(12) Library
(—) Road
(- -) Trail

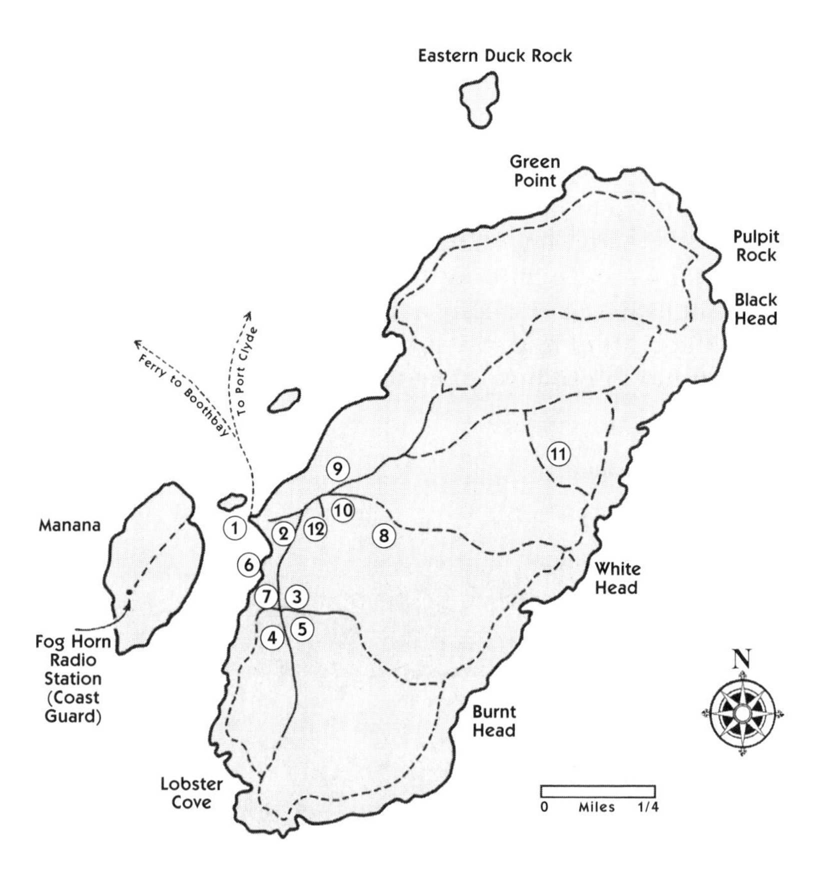

farther two islands thus seen are Monhegan and its smaller sister isle, Manana. They lie like a great mother whale and her offspring well off by themselves in the deep waters of the Gulf of Maine twelve miles out of Port Clyde.

A lobstering community of long duration, Monhegan is also an artists' hideout, an outpost where many of the famous and not-quite-famous come to paint and seek inspiration. Jamie Wyeth has a house that looks south over the rocks here. His father painted on Monhegan as well. Historically, the island's legendary sunsets and sunrises, its rocky cliffs and sheltered harbor have provided a continuous source of ocean motifs and painterly ideas for the many who come to sketch for a day, week, or whole summer. And then there are those who stay permanently. All of the Maine coast engages the eye, but there are scenes on Monhegan that bear capturing generation after generation. Should you disembark from the *Elizabeth Ann* at Monhegan one day without a small easel and paints, you may find yourself in an unexpected minority.

Monhegan has been a point of reference for centuries to sailors, too. Many years ago in his *Pemaquid and Monhegan*, the Honorable Charles Levi Woodbury wrote: "We sailed the next morning, bound east, and on our starboard side, as we neared the point, a lofty island, some leagues away, attracted our attention—it was Monhegan. When we returned from our exploration of the islands of the Penobscot and Mount Desert, we sighted the island, the morning sun, playing on its top, bathed it in light. Amid a peaceful ocean it rose like an island of the blessed."

Some written evidence argues that Norseman Thorwald Erikson may have landed on Monhegan in the spring of 1004. Giovanni Cabotas anchored between the big island and Manana in 1497. He had been given letters patent to the region by Henry VII of England. (A bit of an inconvenience, this, as the pope had already given the island to the Portuguese. How the pope presumed to own it at all remains unexplained.) The island gradually became the nexus of fishing, fur trading, resupply, and ship repair. The Englishman David Ingram anchored at Monhegan in 1569, and Martin Pring, who explored the New England coast extensively, landed here in 1603. Captain John Smith came to Monhegan in 1614, giving the island the appellation Barties, which everyone promptly ignored, preferring the Indian name, which means, quite simply, "the island." Smith gardened on the island and had seven ships built by the harbor. Of his spring garden, Smith noted he had planted it here "in May, which grewn so well it served for salads in June and July."

Monhegan figured as a desirable find for those ships that had survived the long exploratory journey from England. Given its location, Monhegan often was the scene of landfall after the Atlantic ordeal. James Rosier, who arrived in these waters in 1605, wrote: "We descried the land, which bare from us North-Northeast; but because it blew a great gale of wynde, the sea very high and neere night, not fit to come upon an unknowen coast, we stood off til two a clocke in the morning, being Saturday." Rosier describes the island seen: "It appeared a meane high land as we after found it, being but an iland of some six miles compass, but I hope the most fortunate ever yet discovered." A cape here along the coast still bears Rosier's name today.

In 1619, the first permanent settlement on Monhegan commenced. Like many Maine outposts, it provided assistance to the stumbling Plymouth

Monhegan Light

Colony, and our John Smith was a link between the two settlements. The island community saw interruption in 1676 with the hostilities of King Philip's War, just as villages were dissolved on the mainland, settlers fleeing southward. Indians set the island afire in 1689, doing the bidding of the French. When the settlement re-formed, names like Trefethen and Starling were prominent, the grand "pink house" of the Starling heirs later surviving as the Island Inn. Across the harbor, stony Manana had its own hermit for many years. Raymond Phillips lived alone on Manana quite contentedly with a flock of sheep, accompanied otherwise only by ghosts and a tiny Coast Guard station, all of them now long gone.

One of the most famous naval battles on the Maine coast, the contest between the *Boxer* and the *Enterprise* in September 1814, occurred north of Monhegan in the ways between the island and Port Clyde. The Americans prevailed, but two gallant captains perished in the cannon fire. The victory marked one of the last bare-knuckles episodes in Britain's attempt to hold the northern New England coast.

Yale-educated writer William Henry Bishop, then a contributor to *Harper's Magazine* and *The Atlantic Monthly*, came to Monhegan in the late 1870s and in 1880 devoted a *Harper's* piece to the subject of mackerel fishing around the island. Captain John Smith had described Monhegan as "a round, high isle, with little Monanis by its side, betwixt which is a harbor where our ships can lie at anchor." Bishop found little to emend in Smith's description, though in the 1870s a substantial fishing operation had grown and thrived off Monhegan's shores.

Bishop described Monhegan's fishermen as "stalwart, rawboned men in flannel shirts, well-tanned canvas jackets and big boots. . . ." Though his Maine geography was a little askew, Bishop told his readers ". . . Monhegan was the most remote and primitive of all the Maine islands. It had no direct connection with the mainland, and no post office . . . . There were plenty of sheep but little agriculture, no roads nor use for any except to haul a little wood from the other end of the island in winter. In this service cows as well as the few oxen were put under the yoke." The island's openness to light and sea delighted him, and Bishop remarked: "Monhegan had a glorious open out-look, somewhat too rare in the other Maine islands. . . . From an elevated point, [one] could follow the sea all around, and shoreward a distant blue island or two lay in the high-lifted horizon like a cloud over the tops of the pines."

Bishop was moving up the coast, riding with fishermen and visiting the islands as he moved along, learning about those who harvested the sea. He described the appearance of Monhegan's sheltered harbor thusly in 1880: "The little harbor was speckled with small boats when [I] came in, and the schooner *Marthy*, which smacked fresh fish regularly to Portland, and a freighter, purposing to go into Herring Gut to paint, were lying there at anchor. The small boats were tied to the tall stakes, more common as the Bay of Fundy is approached, with crosses on the top, which at low tide give the appearance of a melancholy kind of marine graveyard too. It is not a common kind of harbor. It is a deep channel between Monhegan and Menana . . . open at the outer end and partly closed at the inner by a rugged black ledge known as Smutty Nose. . . . In southeast gales a formidable surf drives in through the passage, and it is then by no means so agreeable a place of anchorage. In a wild night of rain, wind, and pitch-darkness of 1858, the whole contents of the strait, fourteen fishing vessels, besides the flotilla of boats, were piled upon Smutty Nose in a mass."

Present-day Monhegan is a mile-and-a-half-long, half-mile-wide island with one winding gravel main street and several lesser grassy tracks trending off into fog-shrouded spruce and pine. Getting around the island is easier than in Bishop's time. Strollers will see that island architecture has remained quintessentially northern New England, gabled roofs heading away in multiple directions, additions and sheds being common, classic cottage style extending itself to the edge of the woods.

A couple of large old hotels rise in the village, stay-over visits on the island, rebounding from those years when visitors were fewer. There are two, sometimes three small shops and numerous galleries. A delightful, Lilliputian library, founded by

Mrs. John Fremont Hill in memory of two children who drowned in 1926, is open odd hours. Small Fish Beach (or Middle Beach) on the harbor and another beach at the island's north end allow brave swimmers to bathe in very cold Atlantic waters.

Lest this seem merely a place for lazing about, Monhegan's harbor is a working harbor, a small lobster fleet operating here with a strong sense of its own conservation ethic. Since 1907, the community has self-regulated the setting and hauling of traps seasonally so the resource is preserved. "Trap day," usually sometime in early December when everyone is ready, sees great piles of traps taken out and lowered. There they do duty until late June, when islanders haul out a last time until the next winter.

A few years ago, a group of shore-based fishermen, having dragged, seined, trapped, and trawled their own turf into oblivion, wanted to come out to Monhegan to fish it to extinction in their usual manner. Having fouled their own nest, the lads thought it logical to pick Monhegan waters clean. Fortunately, the legislature said no, and the islanders prevailed, their own waters unsullied by such greedy intrusions, their rational approach to conservation recognized.

A walk along Monhegan's main thoroughfare above the docks familiarizes you with the settled west side of the island, shops, church, school, inns, and a gallery or two. Monhegan has its own one-room schoolhouse for the elementary grades. Those older go to the mainland. I cannot recall the school ever having more than eight or ten students in recent years. Ascending to handsome Monhegan Light on a bluff above the village, you find splendid views over Manana toward the mainland, north and west. The protected harbor regularly plays host to overnighting yachts, Monhegan's longitudinal length a reassuring bulwark against the heavy seas of the open ocean.

A network of pretty trails carries the walker to Monhegan's north shore, to soaring Black Head, and through the distinctive old-growth forest in the island's northern center. More trails lead east and south from the lighthouse, first erected in 1824, and then manned by keeper Thomas Seavey. The lighthouse serves as the visual center of the island, and its beam can be seen from various island points if you stroll out in the evening. Its 170,000-candlepower illumination can be seen many miles away in even inclement darkness, and the arc of the light prowls the air mysteriously as its reach atomizes the fog on certain nights.

Originally a bell weighing more than a ton signaled the presence of the two islands from Manana on days and nights of zero visibility. Placed on the lighthouse around 1854, a barely audible foghorn was moved to Manana in 1870 and then replaced by a more efficient Daboll trumpet in 1877, making the hand-operated bell redundant. Monhegan Light was kept by Betty Morrow Humphrey from December 1861 until 1880. Her husband had been appointed keeper in March 1861 but died within

Looking north toward Black Head

months, and Mrs. Humphrey's sons were away serving in the Union army. The light, for its first ninety years, burned whale oil and oil made of animal fat. Monhegan light saw conversion to less malodorous incandescent oil vapor in 1912. A museum in the old keeper's house contains many artifacts of island life and is seasonally open to visitors.

A stroll eastward from Monhegan Light and the Lighthouse Museum leads to exhilarating views over the great 160-foot-high cliffs at White Head. There trails also follow the heights in groves of wind-racked spruce to the island's boulder-strewn southern shore. The rusty remains of a beached coaster lie in that direction. Between the main perimeter trails, a number of well-marked, wooded avenues explore other island backcountry. Several joyous days can be invested in wandering about the hidden corners, cliffs, and forests of Monhegan. (See the author's *Fifty Hikes in Coastal and Southern Maine* for hikes on the island.)

As noted earlier, Monhegan was certainly a known quantity to those who fished, farmed, and logged hereabouts for centuries, but the interesting question of the island's presence in Viking exploration lingers. In a rock cleft on Manana, settlers found an inscribed boulder variously credited to the arrival of the Norse peoples, Phoenician boatmen, Indian writing, latter-day fishermen, or natural weathering. A controversy has both supported and debunked the claims of Norse visits here over the years. Extant Norse records seem to refer to actual sightings of landmarks from around the island. Other researchers claim that the inscriptions are merely accidents of nature. These types of markings also have been seen on the Outer Heron Islands and near Popham, as well as at other sites in southern New England. Similar inscriptions have been found on monuments off the south coast of Sweden. Presently the skeptics reign, despite modern evidence that Leif Eriksson and followers cruised waters in the region from their base near L'Anse aux Meadows at Newfoundland.

Rockwell Kent, Robert Henri, George Bellows, and Andrew Winter were among those artists who painted on Monhegan in modern years. They brought others in their wake. Robert van Vorst Sewell, Marion Monks Chase, James Fitzgerald, Samuel P. R. Triscott, and Mary Townsend Mason worked on Monhegan. Edward Redfield, Edward Hopper, Stow Wegenroth, Leo Meissner, and Fairfield Porter also painted here. Others of regional and national reputation work on Monhegan currently.

Rockwell Kent first studied painting in New York with Robert Henri while undertaking a few limited architectural commissions for which he had an incomplete training at Columbia University. He came to Monhegan in 1905 and made his way here again in 1906 to build a house. He described his first visit to the island in *It's Me, Oh Lord:* ". . . the Monhegan mail boat, the ancient, weakly-powered *Effort,* lies at her Boothbay Harbor wharf in readiness, it would appear—the mail sack having just been tossed on deck and stowed below—to cast off and set sail. And now, the lone passenger having stepped aboard, the motor starts, the lines are slacked and cast off by a loiterer on the wharf, and the *Effort,* slowly, heavily as though to justify her name, gets under way. . . . my eyes are already upon Monhegan as the land of promise, upon Monhegan already risen faint but clear on the far, sharp horizon of the ocean's deep blue plane."

One of the great pleasures of Monhegan beyond its stunning natural character is the circuit of small artists' galleries and studios that exist in and around the center of the village. Open studios are held on varying days of the week in summer, and the opportunity to view work-in-progress and recently completed canvases greets those who take to the back lanes. On any typical summer day, several of these studios are open to view at various points on the island. As you walk about Monhegan, especially on its ocean side, artists are often seen, perched in likely places, capturing the views to seaward. There are probably more easels and paint pots per capita on Monhegan than almost anywhere else in summertime Maine.

Monhegan days drift on with not much sense of the clock, and the visitor would be unwise to think

Monhegan offers hikers unsurpassed scenery.

in terms of schedules. Islands remind us that time is relative, subjective. Days arrange themselves quietly and in consort with prevailing weather. Ultimately, the last boat sails for the mainland, day-trippers depart for places elsewhere, artists shutter their displays, and Monhegan becomes quiet. Only the sound of the sea, working gently, lingers. Fog drifts up from the cold ocean, the lighthouse sending alternate strands of illumination through the moist night air. Dinner is cleared away at the inns. The island paths are shrouded in silent, fragrant darkness. Voices linger briefly over the village as people complete their evening constitutionals. Visitor and resident alike say their final good nights, and Monhegan sleeps.

ACCOMMODATIONS AND MEALS

Most people come to Monhegan for the day, but a fair number stay over, some renting cottages and most staying at the several hotels or guest houses. The **Island Inn** overlooks the harbor; people sit on its front porch and watch the boats come and go. It also boasts a restaurant open to the public. Its rooms have electricity, and some have a private bath. The Island Inn, Monhegan, ME 04852, tel. (207) 596-0371. Toward the south end of the island, opposite the Community Church, the **Monhegan House**, a tall, multistoried Victorian residence, offers forty-five simple, lamplit rooms with shared hall baths and toilets. The Monhegan House also has a dining room open to the public. Daily specials are announced on a board by the front steps. Monhegan House, Monhegan, ME 04852, tel. (207) 594-7983.

The **Trailing Yew**, on a rise farther southward, is an amalgam of buildings with space for sixty guests and the habit of feeding people from other spots on the island as well as its own. If you stay somewhere meals are not served, sign up for your three squares at the Trailing Yew. Eating here is fun because everyone sits together at long tables, and you meet a bunch of interesting people. One morning at breakfast at the Yew, I sat next to a young couple soon to complete a circumnavigation of the United States on bicycles, a Portland restaurant owner, a retired Scottish twosome, a hospital administrator, a German couple, and an artist. The Trailing Yew, Monhegan, ME 04852, tel. (207) 596-0440.

The **Tribler Cottage** rents a single room with bath and several small apartments with private bath and cooking facilities. It nestles against the hillside below the lighthouse and is off by itself on a grassy lane above the library. Owner Richard Farrell takes excellent photographs of the island, which he sells. Tribler Cottage, Monhegan, ME 04852, tel. (207) 594-2445. The **Hitchcock House** uphill on the south end of the island has several guest rooms and cabins seasonally. The Hitchcock House, Horn Hill, Monhegan, ME 04852, tel. (207) 594-8137.

Two small shops on Monhegan's main road offer snacks and sandwiches and a limited grocery selection, with one providing coffee and wine selections. The **Port Clyde General Store**, behind the ferry wharf on the mainland, is open year-round and has sandwiches, beverages, groceries, and other necessaries. Persons renting an apartment or cottage on Monhegan should bring the groceries they require with them.

GETTING THERE

Visitors to Monhegan travel with the **Monhegan Boat Line** out of Port Clyde in St. George. The *Elizabeth Ann* or *Laura B* makes three trips daily to the island in summer, grazing some smaller islands where you are likely to see large numbers of seals resting on the ledges. Two trips daily are made in spring and fall, and the schedule drops to three trips weekly in winter. Reservations are advisable, especially in midsummer and definitely on summer weekends. Monhegan Boat Line, P.O. Box 238, Port Clyde, ME 04855, tel. (207) 372-8848 or www.monheganboat.com. The ***Balmy Days***, a tour boat out of Boothbay Harbor, also offers summer runs to the island, tel. (207) 633-2284.

Penobscot Bay

MATINICUS

As a rather young child, I never spent a Saturday morning eating my pancakes out of earshot of Edward Rowe Snow. An author and lecturer, Snow told stories of lonely islands, the ghosts of shipwrecks, and murder at sea. Come Saturday, like thousands of other children in Maine and New England, I glued myself to the radio, not wanting to miss a word of Snow's stories as they floated across the ether on the Yankee Network. (You will, perhaps, recall a time when there were actually *programs* on the radio, rather than the idiotic garbage that now occupies the commercial airwaves.) Snow had a soft, even shaggy voice plus an acute ability to draw one in as he related tales of ghastly accidents at sea. Or lighthouses growing dark in great storms and heroic attempts to restore the beacon. One couldn't listen to Snow week after week and not become addicted to the coast and islands.

In his popular *Lighthouses of New England*, Snow recounted the history of Matinicus Rock Light and its sister islands. He noted the loneliness of this isolated ledge, its location subjected always to the sea's wild hammering. Aloft, Snow flew over the rock in winter, as he did many offshore lighthouses, dropping sacks of Christmas gifts. With a little effort, travelers to Matinicus today can feast their eyes on both the lighthouse and Matinicus Island, as Snow described them, exploring Maine's most remote island settlement.

The name of this isolated place is in dispute. Matinicus may mean, in Penobscot parlance, a "place of many turkeys." Others have suggested the name comes from the Native term *manasquesicook*, a "collection of grassy islands," or, simply, "grassy isle." At the arrival of Europeans, Matinicus was covered with hardwood groves and some fields, its littoral a grassy verge out to the water's edge.

The message center on Matinicus

Matinicus Harbor

Whatever the origin of the name, the French, Spanish, and Portuguese came early to Matinicus. Spanish coins are sometimes found here even today. The French conducted a fishing station from the early 1600s, but French occupation was transient.

The explorer John Josselyn came to Matinicus in 1638, and visited again in 1671. He spoke well of the island in his journals, saying it was "well supplied with homes, cattle, arable land and marshes." Captain Sylvanus Davis found the harbor occupied by twenty fishing vessels in 1701. William Vaughn set up the fishing station established between 1725 and 1728, but his beginnings were abandoned three decades later after Ebeneezer Hall was killed by Indians in June 1757. Hall had repeatedly

Matinicus

(1) Landing strip
(2) Harbor
(3) Post office
(4) Cemetery
(5) Tuckanuck Lodge
(6) Markey Beach
(7) South Sandy Beach
(8) Community hall /church
(9) Ferry landing

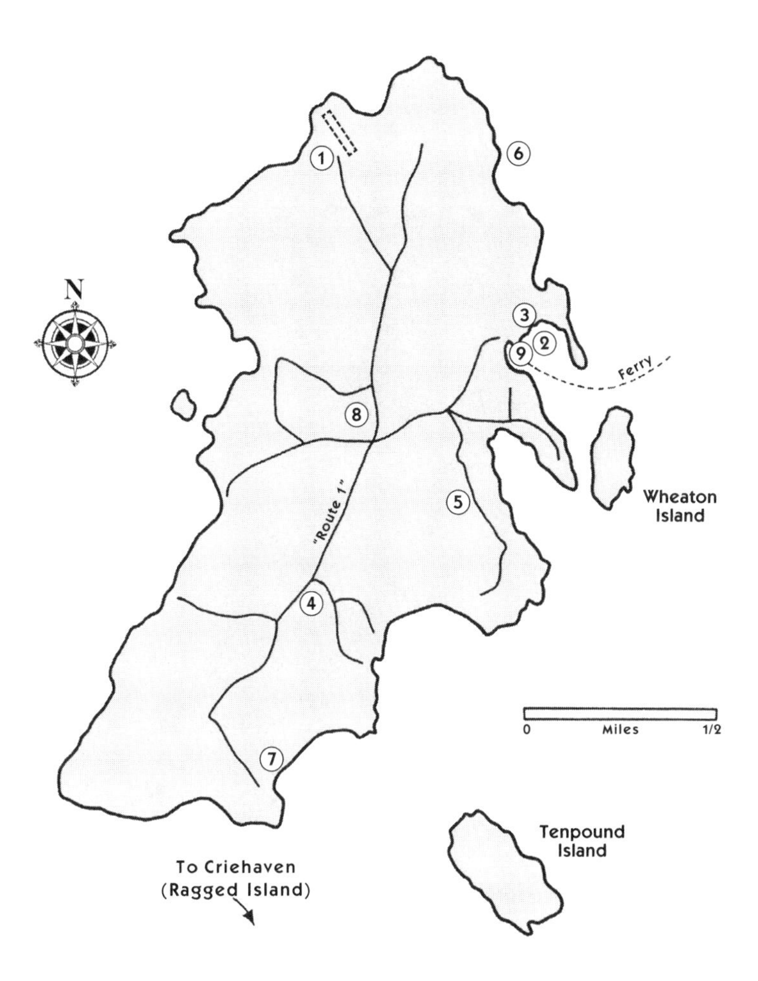

burned over fields and otherwise interfered with the Indians' fishing and fowling, on which they depended for food. He and his son may have murdered a pair of Indians who came onto his land in 1751. Indian leaders petitioned the government for relief from Hall's nuisances, but were ignored. After warnings, they themselves dispatched Mr. Hall uncere-

Community church on Matinicus

moniously, and kidnapped his wife and daughters. Hall's two sons escaped with their lives.

A wooded island, Matinicus measures approximately two miles long and a mile wide. The island once kept in touch with the mainland via mail-boat service, now discontinued. The trip by boat encountered rough seas, fog, and sudden shifts in weather often as not, and the mail could be held up for days. Today the mail flies, whatever the stamp, and visitors to the island get a fine airborne look at the community before setting foot here. On days when the weather prohibits flying, mail and supplies may get to the island on local fishing boats headed out. And then, they may not. The state ferry service runs to the island monthly, and on a more frequent schedule in summer.

A landmass as far out to sea as Matinicus gets no shelter from the mainland. Wind sweeps the island on many days each year, and gales come winter pry at clapboards and roof shingles as boats yank at moorings. A major blow is not an uncommon thing, and one wharfside eating place departed the island in a mean storm in 1978. When stretches of tranquility arrive, islanders treasure the ease of the day and look over their shoulders for the next patch of weather. Fog can establish itself here in summer like a distant relative who has arrived, made a thorough nuisance of himself, and overstayed his welcome. When the island is socked in, air service is suspended.

Matinicus Light, on the Rock, has seen its share

of marauding weather, too. It sits lower in the water than Matinicus itself, and on the other side of Criehaven (Ragged Island). The light's historical record is a litany of frightening episodes. The earliest light tower and keeper's cottage were made of wood, and were soon reduced to splinters by thirty- and forty-foot waves that scoured the ledges. The repaired tower and cottage structures were nearly battered to pieces again in January 1839. The lighthouse service constructed a double-tower stone structure in 1846 with a connecting stone building. This became the home of young Abbie Burgess, who staffed the lighthouse alone in a terrible storm sequence in 1856. While waiting for her father to return from Matinicus, where he had gone for provisions, she kept the light burning for three weeks. Later marrying, Abbie Burgess Grant became the official keeper of Matinicus Light.

People live on Matinicus to fish or lobster, typically the latter, and the island has seen all manner of both over the years. Presently, Island Lobster Company is the sole hub of activity to seaward. Most people on the island have their own traps in waters nearby, and thirty boats in the harbor is not unusual in summer. Supply boats come out from Rockland with support for lobstering and to empty the cars in which lobsters are held for transfer to buyers ashore. In many ways, earning a livelihood in this manner on Matinicus is an extension of a centuries-old tradition begun by those nationalities who used this mound of rock as a way station on their transatlantic fishing expeditions. It may be a tradition in trouble, nonetheless. Though the lobstering has been quite good, federal limits on days spent fishing have generally cast a pall on the New England industry. Still, many are optimistic. Philip Conkling of the Island Institute recently wrote: "For those who stay behind, the devotion to sustaining a way of life that is not for the fickle or weak-willed only gets stronger."

As the well-to-do buy up property on this and other islands, more services are demanded, which places an increased tax burden on those who work

Wheaton Island and Matinicus Harbor

for a living. Native islanders complain of the changes and the potential loss of the traditional island way of life that once prevailed. The cost of delivering electricity and phone service on Matinicus has climbed. The island didn't have phone service until the early 1960s, and reliable, full-time power did not arrive until the early 1980s. Whatever the cost, and even with the winds of change, life on Matinicus is a far cry from the mainland.

It's a tight-knit refuge, too. True island families know one another and their histories so well, they might as well be all one family. As islander Clayton Philbrook told *National Fisherman* reporter Paul Molyneaux not long ago: "I call it multigenerational group therapy. We all know why this one's the way he is, because we knew the parents, and we know what the children are going to be like."

Modern-day travelers to Matinicus fly to the island from Owls Head's Knox County Regional Airport near Rockland. Penobscot Island Air runs on-call air service to Matinicus and two scheduled mail-plane trips each weekday. The journey takes about twenty minutes, weather permitting. The "airport" on Matinicus is a shell-strewn gravel road with no amenities other than a wind sock and the requisite good luck, useful in a crosswind. Air travelers are quite as likely to share their seat with a kitchen sink, boxes of groceries, or a box of spare boat parts on these flights as fellow humans.

Matinicus has a small do-it-yourself lodge for stay-overs, and several island residents rent the occasional room or cottage by reservation. The island has no store or restaurant, so visitors should provision themselves accordingly. Day excursions are easiest, flying out in the morning and being picked up for the flight landward at five o'clock.

ISLAND EXPLORATIONS

The island suits walkers, with woods trails bordering fields of wildflowers, and a rock substrate that burrows to the sea via ledges and promontories in rugged Maine fashion. South Sandy Beach, Markey Beach, and Condon Cove allow sunning and swimming, and there are also beaches on the island's western perimeter. *Exploring ledges and cliffs should be done with great caution.* Rock surfaces are often slippery with algae and rockweed. Waves may cover ledges unexpectedly.

Matinicus is a birder's island, with numerous resident and migratory species in evidence, especially from May to October. Check with Maine Audubon for information on periodic migrations and spottings before departure. At the height of the season, you may identify fifty to seventy-five land-based species in a single day of birding here. A variety of seasonal and resident seabirds will be seen along the island's shores.

For the more adventurous, local inquiries will lead to boat hire for the trip past Criehaven to barren Matinicus Rock, tides and weather permitting. A trip to the Rock ambles by Ragged Island and

Criehaven Harbor and village, a private, summer-only colony immortalized as "Bennett's Island" in the novels of Elisabeth Ogilvie. Off to the east lies low and long Wooden Ball Island. In addition to the lighthouse, the Rock hosts the largest of three puffin colonies on the coast. A state program has been in operation here in recent years to support the puffin colony and reduce the depredations of gulls on these ground-nesting birds. Puffin nesting activity reaches its high point in midsummer. Those hoping to see the puffins are advised to phone ahead to arrange a charter, especially if only making a day trip to Matinicus. Maine Audubon also runs sponsored trips to the Rock.

Matinicus Rock was once the home of the lonely cow Daisy, who probably couldn't figure out what she had done to deserve such isolation. Hauled to the ledge in a sloop that dumped her unceremoniously ashore, Daisy nonetheless did her best to supply the keeper's family with milk. She is said to have been one of only two nonhuman animals on the thirty-two-acre heap of volcanic rock, the other

Matinicus pasture

being a rabbit who eventually died and left Daisy bereft. U.S. president John Quincy Adams appointed John Shaw the light's first keeper in June 1827. Many other families sheltered at the Rock before the light was automated.

On my most recent visit to the island, I flew out on a cloudless day. The views over Penobscot Bay were spectacular, coastal views being a bonus of an airborne visit. A lone sailboat made a slow passage below in the direction of Criehaven, and others moved downwind toward Monhegan. The trip is a direct fourteen nautical miles by air from Owls Head, but a more lengthy twenty-four miles by boat out of Rockland.

After landing at "Matinicus International Airport," I walked along the island's main road, which meanders quietly southward past old farmsteads, the community center and school, and the island's community church. This central road, which some islanders refer to as "Route 1," eventually makes a bend at the village cemetery and runs out in fields and woodlands at the island's southern periphery. The architecture is mainly that typical of older New England farms, Greek Revival here and there and neat Capes, little visited. Some yards sport collections of the old cars and decaying boats often found on islands. In one yard, two ancient pickups lie suspended on mounds of wood and hay as if launched skyward in a fit of pique. My outline was mirrored in pools of rainwater in the gravel track, and a man approaching from the fields remarked on my reflection, "It looked like you were walking on water." I assured him that I'd tried that before, and it hadn't worked.

Near the pretty community church, a cross-island road leads to east and west shores. If you go east, as I did first that morning, you will walk toward the harbor, passing a side lane to Tuckanuck Lodge, the island's only overnight accommodation, and a gift shop and gallery. Farther on, the harbor makes a pretty site, filled with Jonesporters, Novi boats, and the occasional sailing craft. Gulls circle, looking for bits of bait as boats come in with their haul in early afternoon. A great, granite breakwater protects the little bay, and you can walk to it along the rocky shore, staying below the riprap. Walking out toward the breakwater, I went by a battered pickup with a bumper sticker that read "NEVER UNDERESTIMATE THE POWER OF STUPID PEOPLE IN LARGE GROUPS." The tiny post office stands by the wharves, and lobstermen come and go, unloading their catch at lobster cars in the lee of the breakwater.

I asked the postmistress if anyone was serving food to the public on the island. The answer was no, with the exception of Eva Murray, who bakes bread and pastries and serves ice cream and soft drinks in summer. A woman in the post office picking up her mail observed, "We're not a very friendly place, I guess." Both she and the postmistress laughed. The island has a private feeling to it, but people *are* friendly and will say hello or give directions as they pass on the roads. You just won't see many of them.

The postmistress, the person picking up her mail, and myself were the only people in sight. "This is our busiest time of year," the women laughed, musing on our collective solitude. I told my conversants that I was headed out for a walk, and they remarked that I "would probably run into more dogs than people." Such is the solitariness of Matinicus.

I visited the island's two attractive, crescent-shaped beaches, following "Route 1" to its extremities and also exploring the main cross-island road to its western limits. I was in no hurry and enjoyed the water views and the dense coniferous woods wherever I found them. I paused, too, to get a sense of the island's goings-on by reading the notice board at the community's town hall. Following my route, visitors will enjoy ocean views and, if they dare, swimming at South Sandy Beach at the island's southern tip and Markey Beach on Matinicus's northeast border, swimming being reserved for those with very thick hides. Tenpound Island greets the eye not far off Matinicus's southern shore. There are also interesting views toward the mainland at the end of the airstrip. If you explore, you'll find those small, pocket beaches I mentioned on the western periphery of the island, too.

Those who hang about the harbor and wander the jetty will have a good vantage point to watch boat traffic and Wheaton Island, which shelters the harbor. The ferry lands here on the east side of Matinicus on those rare days when it attends. If you've called ahead to Albert Bunker or his successors, an afternoon may be spent chartering a boat for the trip around Criehaven to Matinicus Rock.

After a day of sauntering about and taking the sun, I headed to the airstrip. While I waited for my return flight, a young islander of seven or eight years rode up on his bicycle. He knew all the aircraft that fly out here like trainspotters know locomotives, and told me he hoped his family's grocery order was coming out on the plane. Unexpected guests had depleted the family larder, and they had run out of about everything. The plane arrived and no groceries appeared. Perhaps on the last flight of the day. He hopped on his bicycle and waved as the Cessna 206 lifted me off Matinicus and into the golden, slanted light of the late-summer day.

ACCOMMODATIONS AND MEALS

Some people rent a cottage for a week when they stay on Matinicus, and you will occasionally see FOR RENT signs as you stroll around. Rentals are sometimes shown on the Web under regional real estate rentals, and an inquiry at the post office, tel. (207) 366-3755, well in advance of your stay may produce some suggestions. Sometimes real estate brokers in Rockland handle rentals on the island, as well. A source for names of those currently offering accommodations for rent is the Web site of Penobscot Island Air (www.penobscotislandair.com). For overnighters, Bill Hoadley's **Tuckanuck Lodge** has provided accommodations for years to island visitors who don't expect to be pampered. Here you bring your own sleeping bag, food, and whatever else you can't live without. The lodge provides access to its kitchen and sleeping quarters. Tuckanuck rests on the east side of the island not far from the harbor. Tuckanuck Lodge, Shag Hollow Road, P.O. Box 217, Matinicus, ME 04851-0217, tel. (207) 366-3830.

Island day-trippers should always bring food and water with them, as there are, at the time of writing, no year-round eateries on Matinicus. In summer, stop at Eva Murray's house at the south end of Route 1, turning left at the cemetery. As noted earlier, she sells home-baked goods and ice cream, coffee, and soda in the warm months.

GETTING THERE

Ferry service to Matinicus is most frequent in summer, operating several times each week. For current information and updates on service to Matinicus, call the **Maine State Ferry Service** in Rockland at (207) 596-2202. Crossing time from Rockland to Matinicus is two hours and fifteen minutes. Boats for the island leave from the Maine State Ferry Terminal at the north end of Main Street (US 1) in Rockland. Parking is available here. The ferry terminal is served several times per day by Concord Trailways with connections to Bangor, Portland, and Boston. Service to Matinicus runs only monthly in the off season.

Penobscot Island Air Service lands at Matinicus

Most day-trippers to Matinicus will wish to use the air service from Owls Head. Flight service is provided by **Penobscot Island Air**, tel.(207) 596-7500. Flights to Matinicus depart from Owls Head (Knox County Regional Airport, tel. 207-594-4131) four miles south of Rockland and US Route 1. The Knox County airport is served by commuter air service (US Airways/Colgan Air) from major US terminals. Air transport to Matinicus may be interrupted for hours or days when the sea is blanketed with fog. When one island is socked in, another may be open. Keep your flight plans flexible and go where the weather welcomes you.

The Fox Islands

Fifteen miles due east of Rockland lie the Fox Islands: North Haven, Vinalhaven, Green, and Hurricane, plus many smaller isles in a cluster nearly eleven miles in diameter. The two largest of the group, Vinalhaven and North Haven, look across at each other over the Fox Islands Thoroughfare, a chasm in the bedrock that separated these two bits of raised ground when sea levels were lower. That chasm has long since been filled by the sea. Vinalhaven and North Haven are now distinct communities, the Thoroughfare their common highway.

The Fox Islands were recorded in the logs of many coasting ships. The Bristolman Martin Pring came here in the summer of 1603, the *Speedwell* and *Discoverer* dropping anchor in the midst of this sprawling island collection. Pring is said to have named the islands in recognition of the numerous gray foxes that occupied these isles. He and his crews regularly saw these wily animals raiding nests and fishing along the shore. The Fox Islands lay within fishing grounds heavily used by various European nations, and a modest trade with Indians occurred here, but the islands did not initially see the heavy use that places such as Monhegan experienced. Micmacs (also called Tarrantines or Tarratines), and Maliseets valued the Fox Islands greatly, and, as time went along, repeatedly attacked settlers who attempted to establish permanent island communities. As in so much of northern New England, the real thrust of occupation would come after the 1760s.

Early visitors to the island group were struck by the fine views the isles afforded to landward. Slightly to the northwest, the rangy Camden Hills step along the horizon above the mainland shore, their summits rolling southward toward modern-day Rockland and Rockport. Explorers found these islands well favored with numerous good harbors of their own, and the isles themselves were well placed to do business with the mainland in the years that followed.

Thadeus Carver arrived amid the islands from Massachusetts in 1765, purchasing seven hundred acres of land on Vinalhaven. Carver married a Matinicus woman, Hannah Hall, and together they set about populating the island with their ten children. Settlers, who numbered nearly eight hundred by the time of the Revolution, were harassed by the British, who forced islandmen to help build fortifications or stole sheep from them.

During the years surrounding the Revolution, a shortage of salt also damaged the islanders' ability to pack and sell fish, and the precarious mainland economy could not always support the buying of timber and produce from these island outposts. Life was lived lean in these parts, often for reasons beyond the islanders' control. The Boston legal family of Vinal looked after the island's affairs post-Revolution, and the town took the name of William Vinal even though families such as the Carvers had pioneered here. North Haven and Vinalhaven were held as a single community until 1846.

Vinalhaven and nearby Hurricane Island experienced an economic heyday in the mid-1800s. Granite was first quarried here probably in 1826, the stone used for a house of correction in Massachusetts. New Hampshire granite carver Moses Webster, with his partner George Bodwell, of Maine, initiated the cutting that became the first East Boston quarry on Vinalhaven in 1852. A series of great quarries was developed and mined for the exceptional local granite, and Fox Islands stone found its way into dozens of major buildings in a host of American cities. The largest single block of granite ever quarried in America was cut here in 1899. The 310-ton plinth was sixty-four feet long, and workmen turned it on a giant lathe brought from Boston for the purpose.

Men came from a variety of European countries to bring their stonecutting talents to bear on this rock. The Bodwell Company in its vast operations employed more than fifteen hundred cutters, many teams of workhorses, and nearly a hundred yoke of oxen. The Tillson works on Hurricane became a shore-to-shore company operation. Great skill, agility, strength, and nerve characterized those who put hand and chisel to stone. Much cutting was done manually with thirty-two-pound hammers, which were swung with acrobatic strength, slightly "kissing" the face of the cutter as the hammer whizzed by the head in its downward stroke.

The product of these quarries, such as stone for the New York Stock Exchange, the Library of Congress, Penn Station in New York, and Boston's Museum of Fine Arts, was cut here, rafted down the coast, and then hauled overland to building sites. Whole settlements tied to the granite trade grew up on Hurricane and Vinalhaven. The Hurricane community now sits abandoned, its machinery and buildings overgrown in many places with brush and weed, the island's epoch of exploitation over.

Rockland Harbor and Owls Head

On the way to Vinalhaven, or to North Haven for that matter, the ferry passes the distinctive profile of two important lighthouses, Owls Head and Rockland Breakwater Light. The Breakwater Light was first a shore-based beacon at the point where the breakwater meets the land, built through federal appropriations in the Grover Cleveland administration. Breakwater construction was commenced roughly fifteen years later, and, as the breakwater was gradually extended, the light was moved to its tip. Today this ribbon of fractured boulders is almost a mile long, and a walk out its full length to the light's turret can be an invigorating tonic on a hot summer day. The old keeper's house is now being slowly restored.

The Fox Islands

Rockland Harbor, though today quite active, was once busier still. In the mid-1800s, Rockland was home to a dozen limestone quarries and more than a hundred harborside limestone kilns used to reduce the quarried rock to lime. Nearly a million casks of lime per year made their way out of this harbor on three-hundred-odd ships, bound for ports southward. Two hundred or so more small craft were involved in the cordwood trade, bringing coastal wood from as far away as the Maritimes to Rockland to run the kilns. The business of getting lime to market was a dangerous one. If wetted, lime will burn more or less uncontrollably, and a leaky ship could find itself disastrously afire without remedy. Great care had to be taken to keep the cargo dry.

Farther out while sailing to the islands, Owls Head is seen to the south, its comely lighthouse standing at the apex of this great mound of rock and ledge not far east of Rockland. The eye automatically is drawn to its shape, which rises just south of the lanes. On a tranquil day, the light is strikingly pretty, its black light chamber perched atop a bold white tower, the whole standing on a high bluff surrounded by acres of evergreens.

Owls Head Light has, no doubt, prevented many a shipwreck over its long history; it has also been the scene of numerous tragedies for those unlucky enough to miss its warning. And sometimes those caught in the death grip of the ledges have literally come back from the dead.

Six vessels went aground on these ledges in a

series of storms just before Christmas in 1850. The worst incident involved a sloop that came across Rockland Harbor from Jameson Point. Soon the grounded boat was heavily coated with freezing spray and the three occupants were struggling for survival, their clothing rigid with ice. As the waves threatened to break the sloop to pieces, Lydia Dyer, Richard Ingraham, and Roger Elliott huddled together to conserve body heat, wrapping themselves as one in blankets and oilskins.

As the tide dropped, Elliott, more dead than alive, managed to struggle ashore and rouse the light's keeper. A rescue was effected, and the two frozen bodies of Lydia Dyer and Richard Ingraham were carried ashore, stiff as boards. The two appeared to all eyes quite dead; there were no vital signs, and conversation turned to matters of burial. Among the rescuers were those who would not accept death, however. Local women set to pulling the ice and frozen blankets from the apparent corpses and rubbing the two bodies to promote circulation where there was none. An hour or two passed as despair grew, but suddenly Dyer and then Ingraham began to respond. In a heated room, the ministrations continued, and both gradually recovered, coming back from the dead, as Owls Head people genuinely believed.

The Fox Islands

VINALHAVEN

Ten thousand acres in area, Vinalhaven boasts roughly twelve hundred year-round residents and a substantially larger number in summer. Working islanders are often tied to fishing and tourism. The island centers its activities on Carvers Harbor, where there are shops, galleries, accommodations,

Vinalhaven-style office building

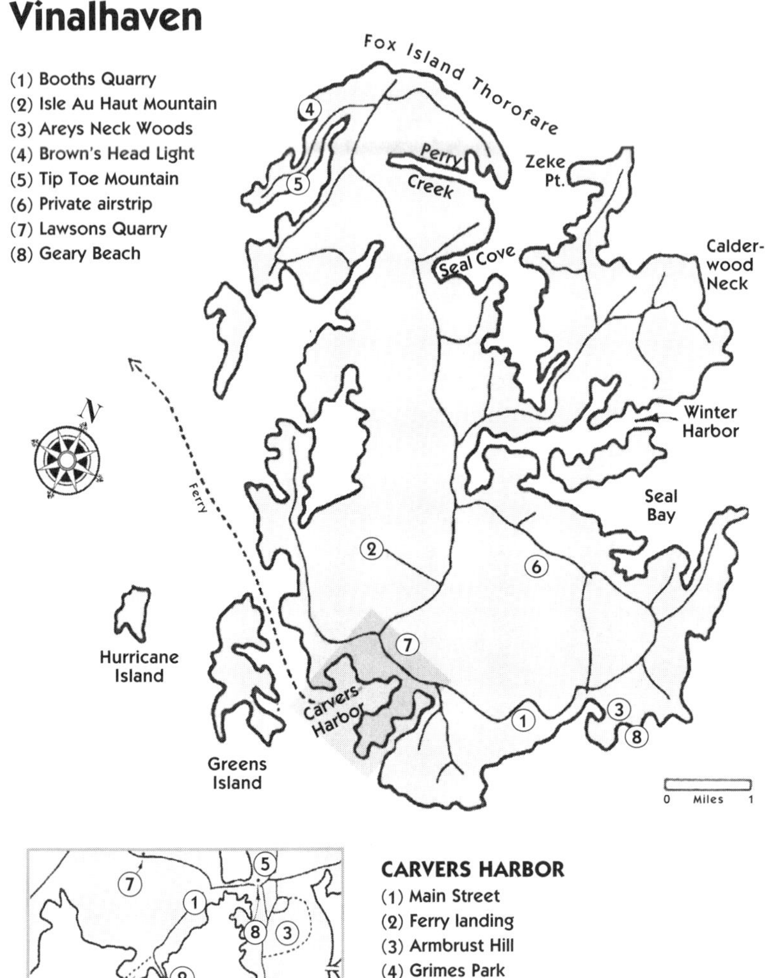

CARVERS HARBOR

(1) Main Street
(2) Ferry landing
(3) Armbrust Hill
(4) Grimes Park
(5) Library
(6) Lane's Island Preserve
(7) Historical Society
(8) Galamander Exhibit

and restaurants. This harbor, one might argue, was the hub of trade and transfer for this and dozens of other islands, large and small, nearly two hundred years ago. Boatbuilding and repair facilities line the waterfront. Rural roads fan out across the less settled wooded areas of the island. Walking the island roads or roaming around the several natural areas on Vinalhaven offers a pleasant escape from mainland life.

The island isn't a place of indoor entertainments, but has much to delight outdoors enthusiasts. Armbrust Hill features hiking trails. Small Grimes Park near the ferry landing has swimming beaches and a picnic area. Freshwater swimming is also possible on Vinalhaven in the Booth and Lawson Quarries. (Visitors should inquire locally and observe all safety measures when swimming.)

Connected by a bridge to Vinalhaven, Lanes Island hosts a partly wooded Nature Conservancy preserve of considerable beauty; its rough fields dotted with spruce offer sweeping water views as they slope downward to ledge and coarse shingle. Areys Neck Woods and Geary Beach also make excellent walking destinations for shoreline exploration. Bicycles and mopeds can *sometimes* be rented on Vinalhaven in summer for those who would venture to the island's northern periphery. Better still, bring your own on the ferry. In the northwestern quarter of the island, a town park rests atop little Tip Toe Mountain, where there are excellent water views. In the same direction, on the

Fox Island Thoroughfare, Browns Head Light stands on a point of land with water views to North Haven and the mainland coast. Pretty Carvers Pond nestles behind the main business section in the village center, its outlet passing below Main Street near the town dock.

Vinalhaven can be visited as a day-return destination if you take a morning boat out from Rockland, returning in late afternoon. Cabin rentals, a year-round motel, and several summer-only and year-round inns offer overnight or longer accommodations by reservation. It is not necessary to ferry an automobile to the island for a day visit. In high season, roll-on and roll-off of an automobile can be a major nuisance, with long lines of vehicles waiting for space on the ferry. Bringing picnic food along is a good idea, or visitors can take meals at island restaurants, snack bars, and take-out places in midsummer. Several grocery stores also offer provisions. Be forewarned, however, that island shops, eateries, and galleries operate on their own eccentric daily and seasonal schedules. It is wise to travel with the assumption that everything is closed and to bring your own lunch, especially at times other than summer.

Cyclists will find the ride northwest along North Haven Road a pleasant means to get to Tip Toe Mountain. Round the Island Road and East Main Street will take riders to Geary Neck and Geary Beach Town Park. Interesting Browns Head Light, which overlooks the Thoroughfare, is near Tip Toe

Mountain on a gravel lane about seven miles from Carvers Harbor. Walkers can pursue these same destinations, or, closer to the center, might stroll out Water Street to Atlantic Avenue. Walking Atlantic Avenue to the south, you'll find a trail to the summit ledges of Armbrust Hill. The short path ascends through pretty spruce woods and leads to several open, granite outcrops. There are views over Carvers Pond inland and out to the open Atlantic from the ledges, and you can picnic there in the pleasant quiet of the island. The trails meander around the summit and work northwest and downward to the island medical center.

A walk farther south on Atlantic Avenue takes visitors to Lanes Island Preserve, where a trail runs through the center of the island and then skirts its

Hiking trail on Vinalhaven

lovely coastal edge. A sand beach graces Lanes' northeast shore. A local map can be obtained at the News Shop, and walkers heading off in almost any direction will find water views and interesting evidence of the great granite plutons that were once quarried here. Walkers and cyclists will find restrooms at the ferry terminal building.

Neighboring Hurricane Island

Hurricane has been referred to as a ghost island, a community that lived and died on granite, its flame now gone out. Today it is home to the Hurricane Island Outward Bound School summer survival-training programs. The island is not open to visiting unless you are participating in an Outward Bound session, but it may be possible to hire a boat on Vinalhaven for a trip around the island; inquire around the waterfront at Carvers Harbor

It was 1870 when former Civil War officer Davis Tillson and two business partners transformed Hurricane into a granite producer like no other. Tilson imported laborers of nearly all European nationalities, erecting three large boardinghouses, stores, and other necessities.

Tilson ruled his island enterprise with an iron hand, his Italian laborers bestowing upon him the name *bombasto furioso*. Workers were expected to patronize the company stores, and failure to do so could lead to dismissal. Tillson also forbade the keeping of animals on the island, creating a little

Carvers Harbor

milk monopoly for himself. He raided the houses of workers to seize rum, leading the *Rockland Opinion* to run columns criticizing him for his kingly absolutism. (A truly helpful man, he even told his workers how to vote.)

Hurricane, regardless of Tillson's energetic despotism, was a lively place, with music and song, parades and dancing. A bandstand was set up for concerts, and islanders constructed a bowling court for nightly games of what the French call *boules*, the Italians *bocce*. People were kept poor on this stony place, but many nonetheless spoke of their years there with a grudging nostalgia and affection. The sheer beauty of the island and its surrounds led those who toiled in the quarries to grow deeply fond of the rocky mound.

In the end, even the merits of island granite could not save Hurricane and its sister quarrying op-

By the harbor

erations. Along came modern formed concrete and the convenience of on-site pouring. Cost-conscious architects and builders became less willing to use cut granite from faraway Maine, and Hurricane stone became a luxury that was seen in fewer and fewer major buildings. By the 1930s, the quarrying boom on Hurricane was over, and the island began its long slide into ghostly remembrance and little more.

MEALS AND ACCOMMODATIONS

Travelers to Vinalhaven will find a variety of island hostelries in and around the village and waterfront, including Rusty Warren's **Candlepin Lodge and Cabins**, which rents four log cabins year-round. The lodge also serves meals in its restaurant and bar, tel. (207) 863-2713. Gail Reinertsen hosts at the **Fox Island Inn at the Moses Webster House**, P.O. Box 451, Vinalhaven, ME 04863, tel. (207) 863-2122 or gailreiner@aol.com. The inn provides complimentary bicycles for guests' use. The **Chatfield House** is a year-round bed-and-breakfast establishment with harbor views, tel. (207) 863-9303 or hschatfield @earthlink.net. The **Payne Homestead at The Moses Webster House** provides bed-and-breakfast accommodations in traditional surroundings. Contact Donna Payne at tel. (207) 863-9963 or payne@foxislands.net. Phil Crossman runs the **Tidewater Motel** at the bridge

Trail over Armbrust Hill

in the heart of the village, tel. (207) 863-4618. Or try Phil Roberts at the **Libby House**, tel. (207) 863-4696. For food service, visit Lonnie and Kathy Morton's **Harbor Gawker/Millrace** in the village, tel. (207) 863-9365. Torry Pratt runs **The Raven,** a seasonal eatery, at the harborside, tel. (207) 863-9365. **Gigi's** is operated by Gabrielle Hatch and is also in the village center, tel. (207) 863-4509. Pam Moore serves at the **Pizza Pit** and sells pizza and snacks, tel. (207) 863-4311.

GETTING THERE

For local information and updates on service to Vinalhaven, call the **Maine State Ferry Service** in Rockland at (207) 596-2202. Crossing time from Rockland is about an hour and fifteen minutes. Boats for Vinalhaven leave from the Maine State Ferry Terminal at the north end of Main Street (US 1) in Rockland. Parking is available here. The ferry terminal is served several times per day by Concord Trailways with connections to Bangor, Portland, and Boston.

If you would prefer to fly to Vinalhaven, contact **Penobscot Island Air** at (207) 596-7500. Air service is provided to Vinalhaven from the Knox County Airport at Owls Head, off ME 73, four miles south of US 1 and Rockland. Service is available on call twenty-four hours a day.

The Fox Islands

NORTH HAVEN

Three miles wide and eight miles long, North Haven is a fifty-two-hundred-acre community of hidden coves and pretty harbors. The island hugs the Thoroughfare, a major avenue of waterborne traffic, and boasts two favored harbors, Southern and Pulpit, both attractive sailing anchorages. The Maine windjammer fleet cruises these waters, and many visitors to North Haven get a brief taste of the island on a weeklong cruise out of Rockland or Camden. Sailboats of all sizes crowd the Thoroughfare in summer, and many islanders race North Haven Dinghies to and fro, while the redoubtable ferry service from Rockland comes and goes, carrying cars and passengers.

Like many Maine islands, North Haven saw use by Native peoples, and there are shell heaps and other remnants of that early civilization here. At what is known as the Turner Site, archaeologists have carbon-dated materials as much as thirty-five hundred years old. Maine State Museum archaeologist Bruce Bourque has cataloged these finds and discussed their significance in his outstanding

Twelve Thousand Years. Indian societies valued the islands of the coast for their fishing and fowling, and fought to keep intrusive Europeans from settling them. Local historian Norwood Beveridge has told the story of those Abenakis who created a great fleet of war canoes, attacking English vessels in the Thoroughfare in 1724. Capturing some watercraft and joined by Micmac brothers, these Natives also headed up the St. George to attack fortifications there. As with other offshore islands in the region, it was not until after the end of the so-called French and Indian Wars and the Treaty of Paris that it was possible for whites to establish a continuing presence here.

One October night in 1836, North Haveners were witness to one of the great tragedies of the Maine coast. A 146-foot side-wheel steamer, the *Royal Tar*, approached the island in a gale on its storm-tossed run from St. John to Portland. Ninety-

Ledges mimic the profile of the Camden Hills to the west.

North Haven

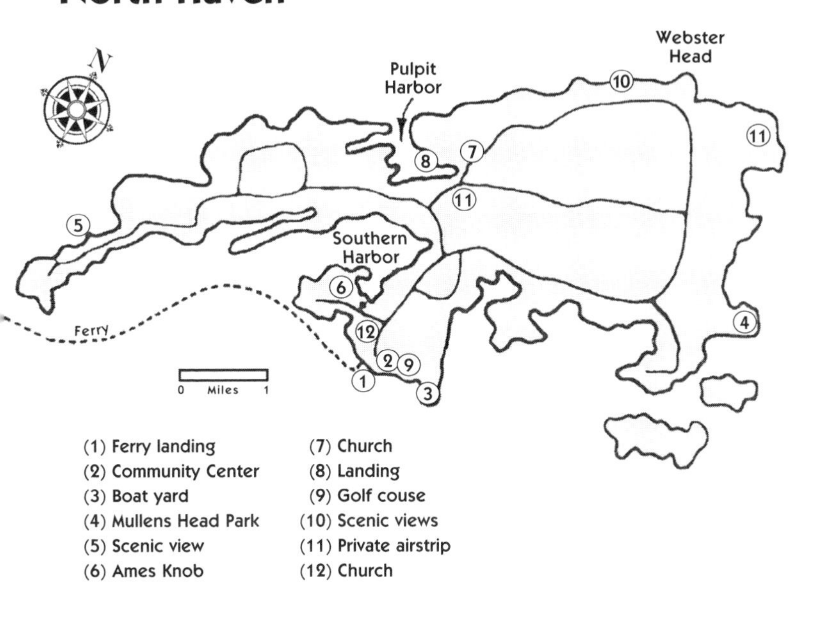

two souls, passengers and crew, were aboard as the ship rolled and pitched southward. According to local stories, battered by the wind and heavy seas, the *Royal Tar* found shelter at the eastern end of the Thoroughfare at Coombs Point and lowered anchor.

It seemed the worst was over, but shortly, the cry of *Fire!* rang out, and the *Royal Tar* was ablaze. Those traveling in steerage often cooked their own meals belowdecks, and they may have accidentally set the vessel on fire. Whatever the cause of the flames, islanders looked on in horror at the pillar of wind-whipped fire and smoke while those aboard stormed the lifeboats as the burning ship went to

Approaching the ferry slip

pieces. The quick appearance of the revenue cutter *Veto* made rescue of forty persons possible, but many of the *Royal Tar*'s human cargo had been lost. They were not alone. Dozens of exotic animals were on the ship, part of a traveling circus, and they were consumed in the flames, too.

North Haven's winding, diminutive Main Street has a post office, library, small shops, a gallery, two restaurants, and, near the wharf, a grocery and luncheonette of uncertain future. A market, the Islander, is on the island's north side near the North Haven Community School. Waterman's Community Center near the ferry dock has coffee, cold drinks, and pastry in season. Island crafts are sold locally, and artists and craftspeople work either year-round or seasonally here, sometimes mixing work in traditional trades with time in the studio. Former Maine legislator Chellie Pingree has had a knitting design business here, selling fine sweaters knitted by local women. (There is presently a shop on Vinalhaven.) As with other, similar outposts, islanders are attempting to expand their tiny economy in ways that preserve island values and sense of community.

In recent years, Broadway producer, director, and set designer John Wulp has been coming over from his Vinalhaven home to support theater in the local school. Wulp and music director Charles Brown Jr. have promoted theater involvement for both local children and adults. Wulp created an island musical several years ago, all roles filled by islanders, and the group got to show their talents off-Broadway. A musical version of *Little Women* was in the works last time I was on the island.

The presence of the U.S. Mail

The old Havens Inn once housed dignitaries who visited North Haven. President Ulysses S. Grant with his vice president, Maine native James G. Blaine, put up here in August 1873. After dinner, Grant and his retinue settled themselves on the inn's front porch and the former general amused his fellows with stories of his experiences in the war years. President Franklin Delano Roosevelt dropped anchor in Pulpit Harbor when steaming down east toward Campobello in 1933 and came ashore briefly. So did Charles Lindbergh, visiting at his in-laws' summer home.

Fox Islanders for decades were dependent on a variety of local operators to supply the islands with

Looking east on Main Street

regular passenger and cargo services to Rockland. A succession of these outfits ran various sail and steam craft to Vinalhaven and North Haven. During World War II, the islands lost their boats when the *W. S. White* and the *North Haven* disappeared into military service. Captain Charles Philbrook, whose name graces a present-day ferry serving the islands, stepped in to carry people and supplies back and forth. Islanders were eventually able to purchase a larger boat. Today the ferry service is operated by the state, carrying autos, passengers, and freight to both North Haven and Vinalhaven.

Those who would stay a little and add to the island's year-round population of about three hundred will find limited overnight accommodations and food service on North Haven today. Visitors will enjoy walking out the island's roads to see what they can see. There are fine views from the road above Southern Harbor and also by Webster Head, as well as around Pulpit Harbor. Easy hiking takes explorers over Ames Knob outside the village for excellent views over the Thorofare. The walk from the ferry to the Knob is about a mile out Main Street and onto Ames Point Road. Also northwest of the ferry landing off Main Street is the short path to little Mount Nebo. A walk out South Shore Road and Mullen Head Road, four miles from the village, brings you to Mullen Head Park, which contains walking paths, a picnic ground, and a swimming area. Campers can pitch tents here with permission from the town office by advance reservation.

The Catholic church on Main Street

ACCOMMODATIONS

On North Haven, **Our Place Inn and Cottages** at (207) 867-4998 offers rentals. For meals, those visiting North Haven should try **Brown's Coal Wharf Marina**, a restaurant on Main Street, tel. (207) 867-4739. In summer, **Waterman's Community Center** by the ferry landing offers beverages and pastry, tel. (207) 867-2100. A seasonal restaurant is open in summer months opposite the Community Center on Main Street. Availability of both accommodations and meals fluctuates considerably with the seasons. It is always wise to call ahead.

GETTING THERE

For local information and updates on service to North Haven, call the **Maine State Ferry Service** in Rockland at (207) 596-2202. Ferry service is provided three times per day to North Haven year-round. Crossing time from Rockland is about an hour and ten minutes. Boats for North Haven leave from the Maine State Ferry Terminal at the north end of Main Street (US 1) in Rockland. Parking is available here. The ferry terminal is served several times per day by Concord Trailways with connections to Bangor, Portland, and Boston.

Air service to North Haven is available on call from **Penobscot Island Air** at (207) 596-7500. Departures are from Knox County Airport in Owls Head, off ME 73, four miles south of US 1 and Rockland. Island flight service is available twenty-four hours a day.

West Penobscot Bay

ISLESBORO

Islesboro lies opposite the Camden Hills in Penobscot Bay, its long, narrow north–south dimension a familiar dark line three miles out on the eastern horizon. It is a wooded place, very rural in flavor, and with limited visible development. Given its long, thin shape, Islesboro often seems all shoreline, its perimeter a collection of superb harbors and coves. From those sheltered inlets, the views from the island's west side back to the mainland are striking, the hills forming a visual border as far as the eye can see. Except at the ferry landing, two markets, two gallery-shop-cafés, and post office, there are few gathering places for Islesboro's roughly 650 year-rounders. The island seems notably reserved, quiet, and private. Islanders like it that way, and seek to keep their domain free of the ugly, honky-tonk clutter found elsewhere.

Islesboro can be explored on foot, on a bicycle, or by car. The short ferry trip accommodates vehicles and cycles, and walkers will find the roads that traverse the island from end to end relatively quiet and not heavily traveled. Seeing *all* of the island matters here—there are so many pretty harbors and

Islesboro

(1) Memorial Museum
(2) Airport
(3) Post office
(4) Golf club
(5) Dark Harbor House
(6) Island Market
(7) Durkee's General Store
(8) Library
(9) Pripet
(10) Town office, school
(11) Historical Society
(12) Tarrantine Yacht Club
(13) Snack Shack
(14) Dark Harbor Shop

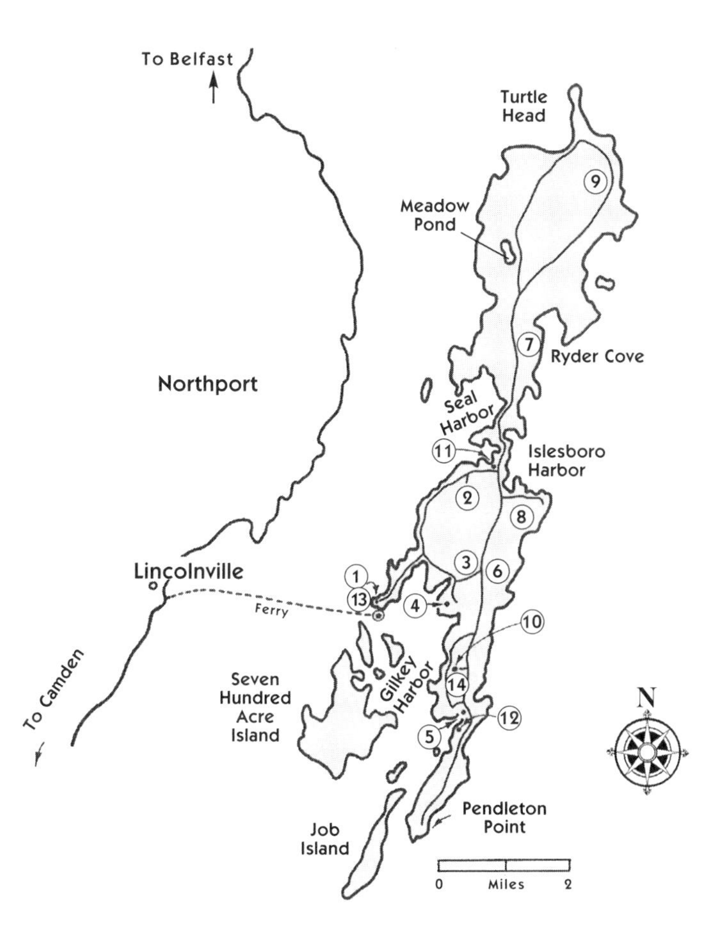

Grindle Point Light

views to landward. At the north end of the island, beautiful Turtle Head Cove offers striking, broad outlooks toward the mainland. Meadow Pond Road brings you south past the pretty body of water of that name. From Main Road you look over Ryder Cove, Sabbathday Harbor, and Seal Harbor. Crew Cove and Islesboro Harbor are at the Narrows and are equally attractive. Derby Road and Pendleton Point Road carry you out to Pendleton Point, where a town park offers outstanding views east and south. Fishing boats hauling traps work these waters daily around Job and Lime Islands. Sailors find these channels inviting, too, and craft under sail move up and down the waters from Gilkey Harbor on fair days.

Islesboro

The southern end of the island, known generally as Dark Harbor, embraces a large colony of classic "cottage" homes, a colony of seasonal expatriates whose forebears began to settle here more than a hundred years ago. These in-migrants were hardly Islesboro's first occupants, however. Fishermen, particularly those from Block Island, Rhode Island, came up the coast and stopped at Islesboro for drinking water and fuel. Hearing of the island's virtues, Massachusetts Bay residents commenced settlement in the 1760s on what charts then termed Long Island. Southern New England whalers used the island as a depot in the 1850s.

Channel traffic

Pendleton Point shoreline

With British naval permission, Harvard researchers led by Fortescue Vernon came to these waters in October 1780 to scientifically record the solar eclipse. Despite the ongoing Revolution, the British allowed the Harvard group to go ashore on Long Island in the name of science. Shubael Williams, an islander, sheltered the expedition and provided its members with essentials, despite British orders of nonfraternization.

Islesboro saw formal incorporation in 1788, the town including Long, Lasell, Lime, Seven Hundred Acre, and Marshal Islands. Long Island today is most commonly referred to as Islesboro even though the name once applied to all the islands collectively. Much of the big island's original cover was gradually removed; the forests were cleared as farms supplemented income from fishing. The faded remnants of these smallholdings sometimes can be found in the woods that have returned to again blanket the island in the present. Ancient graveyards, their angled stones barely legible, still linger in the new growth. The main island enjoyed rich clam beds along its shores, and clamming became an industry for a while, a cannery being set up. Signs of commercial enterprise beyond those that are traditional are few on Islesboro today.

Harvard connections have long played a role in island settlement. Crimsoner Peter Brackett acquired two hundred acres in the Dark Harbor area in the 1880s and invited friends from established families to join him. The Islesboro Land and Improvement Company was formed and soon owned the southern third of the island, complete with magnificent hotel. The colony of "cottages," twenty- or thirty-room houses complete with servants and grounds staff—grew apace until Dark Harbor became its own little community of the privileged. I noticed one of these cottages for sale recently at a price of $7,800,000. How many would you like?

In Islesboro's heyday, American illustrator Charles Dana Gibson came here and purchased most of nearby Seven Hundred Acre Island, from which earlier settlers had chased a native Indian community. The nationally popular artist continued to visit the island with his family until 1944. President Theodore Roosevelt, Lord and Lady Astor, and other notables visited Islesboro, too. Some of the island's long-term, seasonal habitués convert their affection

Grindle Point Light from shore, ferry landing at right

Looking toward the Camden Hills from the western shore

for Islesboro to a permanent thing and retire here. The big island today remains a quiet haven, rather more like a neighborhood in Newport, with life lived pretty much at home.

For visitors who arrive by ferry, having a car or bicycle along is essential. With either, a tour from the west center of the big island to the sweeping cove at its north end and back can be made at a leisurely pace. Another tour takes you south past island shops to Pendleton Point, where you can walk along the shore by the wooded promontory. There are picnic tables and fireplaces here for those who would linger while waiting for the return boat jour-

Turtle Head Cove

ney to the mainland. The nearby lighthouse next to the ferry landing also merits exploration.

ACCOMMODATIONS AND MEALS

The cottage-style **Dark Harbor House** offers traditional rooms seasonally. Accommodations are simple, television is banned, bathrooms are shared. Several rooms have fireplaces. Dark Harbor House, Jetty Road, Islesboro, ME 04848, tel. (207) 734-

6669. The **Dark Harbor Bed-and-Breakfast** offers rooms at 119 Derby Road. Call (207) 734-9772.

The seasonal **Snack Shack** vends sandwiches and burgers by the ferry landing. The **Island Market**, operated by David and Linda Mahan, is in the center of the island and offers sandwiches and beverages plus other necessaries. The market is open six days a week, and Sundays as well in high summer, tel. (207) 734-6672. **Mary's Kitchen** is a deli and lunch counter at Durkee's Market on the northern end of the island. Toward the southern end, the **Dark Harbor Shop** serves light meals, sandwiches, salads, and ice cream.

GETTING THERE

Maine State Ferry Service to Islesboro departs from the terminal at Lincolnville Beach on US 1. The *Margaret Chase Smith* makes seven to nine round trips daily, depending upon the season. Call (207) 789-5611 for local information during normal business hours. The short journey takes about twenty minutes. When purchasing your ticket, be sure to reserve space on a specific return trip if you are transporting a car.

On-call air service to Islesboro is available via **Penobscot Island Air** at (207) 596-7500. Departures are from Knox County Regional Airport in Owls Head, off ME 73, four miles south of US 1 and Rockland. Air service is available twenty-four hours each day.

East Penobscot Bay

ISLE AU HAUT

A continuing argument might be waged as to precisely *where* Maine's coastal islands are the most resistant to the twenty-first century. One could argue that *any* coastal island is an improvement on the depredations of mainland shopping malls, superhighways, and media noise. Absolutely. Still, I observe that, as one works northward along Maine's glaciated shore, communities get smaller, the effects of modernity less noticeable, and the islands still more serene and unalloyed. All of the Maine coast

Stonington Harbor

pleases the eye, but as one drifts farther down east, human intrusion fades and, in places, nearly disappears. Where a human presence is felt at all, it is seemly, tied to traditional occupations, and deeply anchored. My mother came from this country. And her parents before her, her mother making the leap from Grand Manan Island to a little mainland farm as far down east as you are likely to get.

I am speculating here about that country which thrusts itself into the eastern end of Penobscot Bay and then eases north and east, as if pushed along by a prevailing wind, as were so many ships here in their time. Connected places such as Deer Isle and Stonington support a quiet mix of fishermen and artists. Spruce-clad islands interlaced in a field of dense blue lie offshore, one of the most beautiful places in the world to hoist sail and beat downwind or to point one's kayak toward blue water.

Here, too, is Isle au Haut, a place of near six thousand acres, almost half of which are in lands of Acadia National Park. The island is six miles long and less than half that wide, a hilly place of low summits and wooded paths that climb from the sea to striking lookouts. Pretty Long Pond offers fresh water on the island's ocean side near Horseman Point, its waters reportedly stocked with trout and salmon. In the surrounding seas, five small islands are distributed just offshore, like vigilant sentries at Isle au Haut's corners. York Island lies to the east opposite Mount Champlain, bordering the channel known as the Turnip Yard. Burnt Island lies to the

The Thorofare

north and Kimball Island to the northwest across the thorofare. Eastern Ear and Western Ear rise to the southeast and southwest, respectively. And then there are all those interesting little offshore formations such as South Popplestone Ledge, Little Spoon Island, and Sheep Thief.

Around 1600, the French and English set about contending for control of the region. The island acquired its name from Samuel de Champlain, who sailed these waters south of *les Isles des Monts Desert* in 1604. Nonetheless, European settlement did not occur continuously until the late 1700s fol-

Isle au Haut

(1) Isle au Haut Thorofare
(2) Point Lookout
(3) Mt. Champlain
(4) Village of Isle au Haut
(5) Ranger station
(6) Thunder Gulch
(7) Eastern Head
(8) Head Harbor
(9) Western Head
(10) Campground
(11) Duck Harbor ferry landing
(12) Ferry (town landing)
(13) Robinson Pt. Light and Keeper's House
(—) Paved road
(– –) Unpaved rod
(- - - -) Hiking trail
( ) Acadia National Park

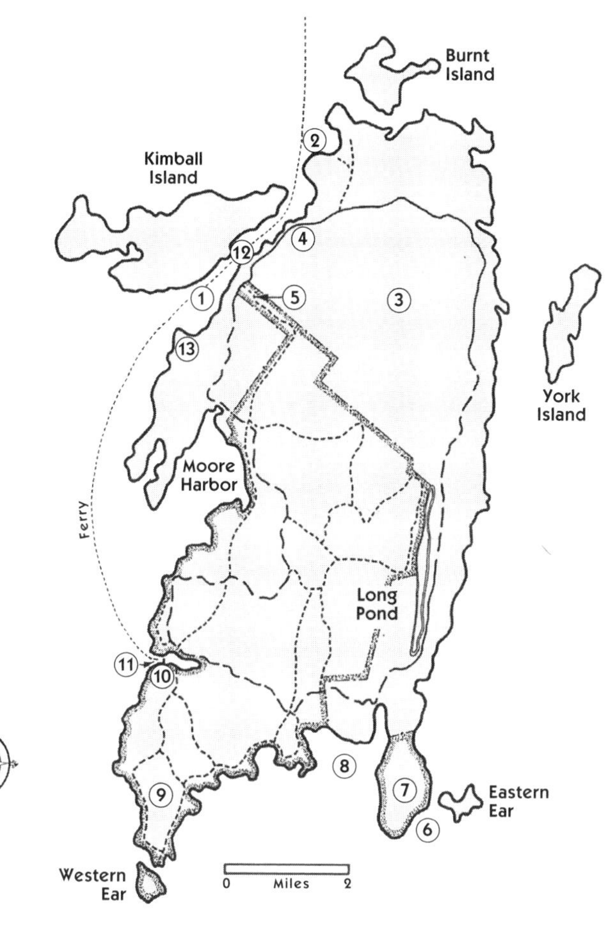

lowing the long series of Indian–European conflicts that dogged New England during and following King Philip's War. The Barter family of Booth Bay, led by Peletiah Barter, are believed to have been the first long-term settlers, arriving in 1792. As on other islands of its size in the region, fishing, farming, and boatbuilding were occupations here. A saltworks, sheep grazing, and shipping emerged as island occupations. Lobstering became part of the island economy in the 1860s. A cannery was constructed, and catches from island waters were shipped to Boston, New York, and London. Stories record that lobsters were so plentiful along the island's shores, residents could clamber about at the riprap, capturing them with hand nets in tidal pools.

The Bowditch family of Salem and Boston, with Albert Otis of Belfast, organized a sort of colony on Isle au Haut. They invited friends in the Boston and New York business community to join them on the island at what became the Point Lookout Club. The group's periodic philanthropy provided a number of amenities for the island and occasional employment for islanders on those projects the club supported. A large chunk of the club's substantial island holdings became a unit of Acadia National Park in the mid-1940s through the generosity of Ernest Bowditch's heirs.

Today Isle au Haut is a rather private place of attractive homes in the vernacular architecture of the Maine coast, homes often used only seasonally. A small fishing community anchors the settlement year-round; a national park center has been established here also. There's a lighthouse, too, built in 1907, that offers limited numbers of guests gourmet dining and sleeping rooms amid unusual surroundings. By reservation, hikers will find primitive lean-to accommodations or tent platforms at the national park site at Duck Harbor, four miles south of Isle au Haut's village center. There are otherwise only a couple of public hostelries on the island, and, unless you have a boat or hire one in Stonington, Isle au Haut is best visited by coming out on the first mail boat (year-round) or Duck Harbor Tour Boat (summer only) and returning on the last trip made by either later in the same day.

Jeffrey Burke, with his wife owner and innkeeper at Isle au Haut's converted lighthouse, has written of his family's decision to become working Maine islanders. "I never asked for this life—living in a run-down lighthouse on a rocky island off the coast of Maine; taking in a procession of strange travelers to pay for its renovation. It simply fell in my lap. . . ." Burke goes on in his *Island Lighthouse Inn: A Chronicle* to describe the awful challenges and thorough delights of making a go of it in such an outpost. His and his wife's story is must reading for anyone who thinks creating and operating a successful island hostelry is a cakewalk for the bored.

The island's great attraction, of course, is its quiet natural beauty and relative freedom from development. Isle au Haut's mountains are gentle and can be climbed by any well-shod person who is reasonably fit. These uplands lend the island a distinctive profile when you gaze to seaward from the summits of the Camden Hills. Isle au Haut trails take you through deeply wooded lowlands to ledgy outlooks with splendid views. Experienced hikers may be tempted to traverse the island's long north–south ridge, comprising 554-foot Mount Champlain as well as Sawyer, Jerusalem, and Bowditch Mountains. There are other peaks and trails that can be walked singly. The terrain is rough enough despite the low elevations, and walkers should plan accordingly. Hikers can also make a complete circuit of the island on a combination of paved and unpaved

Ferry landing at Isle au Haut

roads and trails. Isle au Haut is not a place of manicured parkways.

ACCOMMODATIONS

Day-trippers to Isle au Haut may wish to arrive in Stonington on Deer Isle the evening before in order to be on hand for the first boat to the island in the morning. There are a number of motels and guest houses on Deer Isle. Most are seasonal but several are open year-round. Check with the Deer Isle–Stonington Chamber of Commerce at its Web site: www.deerislemaine.com.

For those who wish to spend a night or two or three on Isle au Haut, there are several choices. Summer hikers and kayakers who enjoy camping will request an advance reservation form from the **Acadia National Park** authority, (207) 288-3338. This number also provides weather and trails information. See also www.nps.gov/acad. Isle au Haut camping reservations can be made by mail beginning on April 1 of each year. The park camping area on Isle au Haut is several miles south of the village on the west side of the island. It features five lean-to shelters. You may also pitch a tent, but it must fit under the canopy of a lean-to. These are carry-in, carry-out campsites, and campers must take their trash back to the mainland with them. Maximum stay is three nights from mid-June to mid-September and five nights in the shoulder season. There is a modest fee of $25 per permit.

Three establishments take overnight guests on Isle au Haut as of 2005. As noted earlier, Jeff and Judi Burke operate the **Keeper's House** at Robinson Point. This attractive lighthouse-*cum*-inn offers four guest rooms and a tiny cottage from late May through October. There is no electricity, and rooms are lamp- or candlelit. The cottage, once the lighthouse's oil storage building, is off by itself and requires a bit of a walk to showers. Three meals are provided, and local recipes and baking are specialties. The lighthouse, around since 1907, is now a living museum. The Keeper's House has bicycles for guests to use, too. Visit www.keepershouse.com or write: The Keeper's House, P.O. Box 26, Isle au Haut, ME 04645.

A fine old mansard-roofed house is the **Inn at Isle au Haut**, operated from June through September by Diane Santospago. The inn rents four rooms and provides breakfast, a picnic lunch, and imaginative dinners. Bicycles are available for guest use. Contact www.innatisleauhaut.com or write: The Inn at Isle au Haut, P.O. Box 78, Isle au Haut, ME 04645.

Try also **Bel's Inn**, a former local captain's house, which rents two bedrooms with shared bath. The inn looks out over the Thoroughfare between Isle au Haut and smaller Kimball Island, and serves three meals each day to guests. Bel's Inn, 612 Seaside Harbor, P.O. Box 61, Isle au Haut, ME 04645, tel. (207) 335-2201.

Sometimes when booking island accommodations, rates may seem expensive. Note, however, that rates in facilities such as these include accommodation for *two* people plus *three* meals per day for *two* people on an island where most foodstuffs must be transported from the mainland. Under such circumstances, rates are actually quite reasonable.

Readers will get a sense of place from recent books tied to island life hereabouts. Jeff Burke's *Island Lighthouse Inn: A Chronicle* has already been mentioned. Linda Greenlaw, an Isle au Haut person and captain, has written several books on fishing and island life, including *The Hungry Ocean* and *Lobster Chronicles.* Peter Scott is author of two nov-

els with island references here, *Something in the Water* and *The Boy Who Came Walking Home.*

GETTING THERE

Boat service to Isle au Haut leaves Stonington on Deer Isle daily except Sunday. The Isle au Haut **mail boat**, *Miss Lizzie*, carries passengers and cargo at least twice daily to the island. Extra trips may be made in high season. Reservations can be made by phoning (207) 367-6516 or (207) 367-6503. Day visitors would do well to take the 7 A.M. or 11:30 A.M. boats outward in summer, returning to shore at 5 P.M. Paid parking is available at the **Stonington Dock Company**. Bicycles and kayaks may be carried to Isle au Haut for an extra fee.

Isle au Haut ferry landing

East Penobscot Bay

DEER ISLE

Isle au Haut is gained via another island, Deer Isle, where travelers arrive by crossing the soaring suspension bridge over Eggemoggin Reach. Deer Isle itself is an interesting haunt and worthy of description even though one does not have to board a ferry or plane to reach it. Visitors will pause at the tiny village of the same name on the island's northwest corner and then proceed to the larger village of Stonington on a splendid harbor to Deer Isle's south. Deer Isle first thrived on fishing, boatbuilding, and quarrying, and many Deer Isle men sailed the world. Being at sea was sufficiently dangerous that many never returned. One census recorded that there were one hundred mariners' widows on the island in 1886. And there existed, perhaps, that many again who had remarried after losing a husband to the sea.

Deer Islanders showed their displeasure over attempts to render their island more or less "dry" in 1830. Maine was swept by periodic efforts to render it pure and spirit-less throughout the nineteenth century, and the island did not escape the teetotal crusaders. A kind of partial temperance was enforced, and the habitually inebriated were prevented from buying their daily intake at local purveyors. Those who vended liquor were threatened with loss of licenses if they sold spirits to the island's determined drunks. This rush to godliness went against the grain of many a seaman, who liked to determine his own measure of rum.

In 1830, a belligerent opponent of drink informed on two spirit merchants who were ignoring the rule as they cheerfully offered liquor to any who could stagger in and pay for it. These two merchants were hauled into the courts while committed teetotalers loudly rejoiced. Those who favored unlimited drink were, on the other hand, not amused. As the informer emerged from the assizes after testifying, a riotous mob set upon him, giving the man a generous, well-applied beating. He managed to escape with his life through the agency of several rescuers. Those who meted out his well-merited thrashing were never sentenced, and the great Deer Isle Liquor Riot of 1830 passed into history.

Deer Isle is sparsely settled and not unpleasantly touristy. Much of the island is rural and wooded, its shores in the midst of an exceptionally attractive section of the coast. Stonington has been recently discovered, but still is a Maine place, especially oriented toward fishing, and boasting a harbor perfectly suited to that enterprise. It is also a place to which artists come and, often, stay permanently. The islands off Deer Isle that lead southward are a favorite venue for sea kayakers, the route providing some of the finest glimpses of the coast available to paddlers.

On the back road from Stonington to Deer Isle, ME Rte 15, hikers will find Crocket Cove Woods off Whitman Road. A Nature Conservancy property, the woods offer interesting and easy nature trails through what has been called a "fog forest" of the first order. (See the author's *Weekend Walks Along the New England Coast* for hiking information.)

ACCOMMODATIONS AND MEALS

All of Deer Isle is worth exploring, on your way either to or from Isle au Haut. Day-trippers to Isle au Haut may wish to arrive in Stonington on Deer Isle a day or two before venturing to the outer island not only to be on hand for the first boat outward in the morning, but also to explore Deer Isle itself, which provides many fine saltwater views of the Atlantic and the islands. There are roughly twenty motels and guest houses on Deer Isle, most seasonal but several year-round. There are shops, galleries, and restaurants in Deer Isle Village at the top of the island. Farther down ME 15, Stonington offers both accommodations and places to eat, and also more displays of local artwork. Kayak rentals and services are available locally. Check with the Deer Isle–Stonington Chamber of Commerce at its Web site www.deerislemaine.com for information and reservations.

Jericho Bay

SWANS ISLAND

South-southwest of Mount Desert Island, Swans Island floats in the Atlantic, looking from the air like a giant dinner roll out of the middle of which an enormous bite has been taken. A largish six-thousand-acre island amid many smaller ones, Swans perches at the mouth of Blue Hill Bay, awash in muscular, conflicting currents. It is a hilly, ledgy, sometimes even marshy island with serrated north and south shores that greet regular eleven-foot tides, rising to sixteen feet on a spring full moon. Now and then, the tides around Swans have been described as violent. Periodically, they are bolstered by the swift currents that roam from east and northwest, and the wind ruffles the dense, spruce feathers of the wooded island sometimes no less energetically than the sea.

A necklace of other islands supports Swans to the south, east, and west, shaping if not mitigating the strength of local currents. Placentia, Black, and Great and Little Gott Islands lie a mile or so off Swans to the northeast. Tiny Sheep and Eagle Islands plus Pond, Opechee, and Black stand across

Swans Island

(1) Ferry landing
(2) The Carrying Place
(3) Buswell's Cabins
(4) Burnt Coat Harbor
(5) Sea Breeze Restaurant
(6) Library, museum
(7) Grocery store
(8) Quarry pond
(9) Fishermen's Coop
(10) Motel / bike rental
(11) Lighthouse

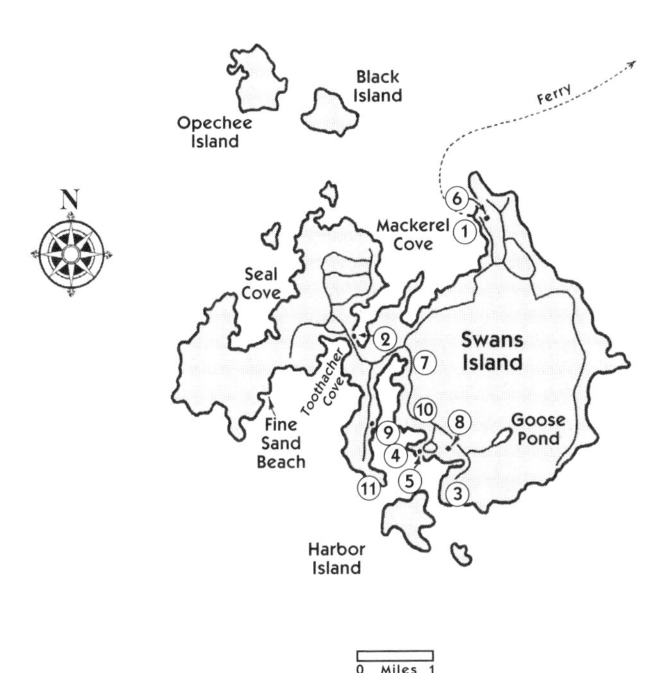

the Casco Passage opposite Swans Island's northwest corner and Marshall and Seal Coves. Long Island (Frenchboro) lies to the southeast. Marshall

Island is the largest of its kind to the south, separated from Swans by Toothacher Bay.

Between the bay and Mackerel Cove, Swans narrows to a mere causeway, its western limits attached to the center of the island by no more than a thread. Swans admits the ocean farther in Burnt Coat Harbor, around which the village of Minturn has grown up. The narrow, mile-and-a-half-long pocket makes an excellent haven for fishermen and has been referred to often as one of the finest natural harbors in Maine. Just at the mouth of the bay, monitoring the channel, is Burnt Coat Harbor Light, perched on the ledges of Hockamock Head.

The mountains of Mount Desert rise magnificently not far away to the north, catching the sun

Meetinghouse on Swans

Burnt Coat Harbor Light at Hockamock Head

with their exposed, glowing pinkish granite. A perpetually busy sea lopes up Swans Island's hidden coves, the rock crevices of Benny's Den and Spouting Horn whumping and sighing with each stiff comber. The island's east and west shores are wooded, spruce cover extending itself out on the ledges, interrupted occasionally by shingle beaches of ocean-candled rock worked regularly by the tide. Beyond the shingle there are large boulders, fractured, rough things of beauty, but unfriendly to those afoot. Walking is best at slack tide.

Not all of Swans hugs the sea. There are those places where, in its eastern lands, the island rises. Two-hundred-forty-foot-high Goose Pond Mountain shelters an attractive four-acre pond of that name, and Big Mountain is in the same neighborhood. They save the topography from flatness and are visible offshore as handsome additions to the island's profile. Hikers and cyclists can explore roughly thirty miles of roads on Swans, often finding outstanding water views as they proceed. Distinctive Fine Sand Beach lies on the west side of Toothacher Cove, a spot worth exploring and reached via a half-mile foot trail off West Point Road. A pretty shingle beach is on the north end of Toothacher Cove adjacent to the Carrying Place, the narrow sand- and *Rosa rugosa*–strewn strip that connects the island with its westernmost turf.

"Low-drain" (or "low dreen") tides here on the new moon not only build to impressive heights, but scour the coves and depart, leaving the shoreline beached and high and dry. This can be convenient if you want your boat to stand dry on its keel while you do below-waterline repairs. A low-drain tide is less salutary when you've moored close to the ledges and have a wait of many hours before your cove refills and you can get under way. And then there is the weather itself. Sailors, once at sea, may find themselves contending with major shifts in weather that often follow extreme tide activity around Swans. This is no everyday place.

Swans boasts a long history of human activity, its European discovery often credited to Samuel de Champlain, who coasted these waters in the summer of 1604. He is said to have given Swans the name *Brûle-Côte*, which was later anglicized to Burnt Coat and sometimes to Burnt Coal, which has stuck in similar form as name to the harbor. The largest of the three island villages, Minturn, has grown up along the east side of this water, and there are shops and stores here and at the village of Swans Island on the west side of Burnt Coat Harbor, where fishing wharves collect the day's catch. This perfect harbor saw use by the migratory fleets of various European nations from the time of its discovery. The island had been a place of hunting by aboriginal tribes even earlier. Maliseets frequented these islands, and relics of their passing have been found here.

The island takes its modern appellation from Colonel James Swan, a native of Scotland's Fifeshire, who came to America at the age of eleven, Fife seeming, one guesses, even more desolate and unpromising than Maine's unfamiliar coast in winter. The young Swan, wanting something more than just haggis in his future, set to making his fortune in New England, most notably in Boston. A friend, later, of General Knox, he bought the Burnt Coat Isles in 1784. Swan was a jack-of-all-trades, possibly a fomenter of the Boston Tea Party, and sometime adjutant general in the Massachusetts-Maine militia. He is said to have made a fortune in Massachusetts and Maine real estate and hoped, it is certain, to do the same with his islands.

The forested island saw much cutting under Swan's tenure, sawmills and gristmills were established, and fishing became an economic staple. In time, Swan exceeded his financial tether and went bankrupt, fleeing to France, where he was imprisoned for debt. He might have regained his freedom by simply acknowledging the debt, but he argued

Traps at the ready

the claim was false and refused to plead. Swan is said to have once brought Talleyrand to the island, but he himself would not manage to see it again in this life after his French imprisonment. His detainment, probably on trumped-up grounds, lasted from 1808 to 1830. Barely a year after being freed, Swan died in Paris, a disappointed fellow.

After Swan's demise, the situation on the island disintegrated, with ownership of various plots all in a tangle. Squatters' rights were invoked, and those who had established themselves formed a self-regulating community. David Smith, the first permanent settler on the island after the Revolution, rose to prominence in the island's governance and was deferred to willingly by settlers as "King David." (There may have been a certain affectionate nostalgia in this, so soon after the Revolution.) A man of appetites and given to bear hunting, Smith reportedly amused three wives and fathered twenty-four children. In subsequent years, Swans prospered as a fishing community with outstanding catches of mackerel, herring, and lobster. It is a busy lobstering island still.

Long blessed with an aura of separateness, Swans has begun to change. In the mid-1980s, three major developments were approved and construction commenced in a gradual sort of way. Islanders seem divided on the benefits of building in-comer housing. Some believe growth spreads the tax burden and supports island services, while others feel it guarantees higher taxes to pay for new services, plus altering the feel of community here. This debate troubles many island communities today and won't easily be resolved.

Visitors will find the **Library and Museum** adjacent to the ferry landing interesting. It sports a collection of traditional tools, Indian artifacts, spinning wheels, and books reflective of island life in yesteryear. Hours of operation vary. Information available at www.swansisland.org or call (207) 526-4330.

Minturn has a swimming place at a granite quarry where granite steps lead to water considerably more pleasant to swim in than the ocean. Hikers should ask locally for directions to the summit of **Big Mountain**, where there are fine water views.

Those arriving on their own boats will find a variety of services in the island's harbors. Gasoline and diesel are available on the west side of Burnt Coat Harbor at the **Fishermen's Coop**. There are boat repair and storage facilities here, too. Look also for yachters' facilities at **Harborside Market**, including showers, a Laundromat, and food service in the village of Swans Island. There are dinghy floats in the harbor, and users should ask permission.

Away from the harbor and the ferry landing, Swans remains a quiet, wooded place. Perry Westbrook in his *Biography of an Island* noted that Swans supports hares, red and gray squirrels, muskrats, and deer. Alongshore, porpoises, otters, black shags, sea pigeons, eiders, fish crows, several gull species, and the rare whale are spotted. Hawks are seen here, too, during seasonal migrations. The island remains a handsome place of great natural beauty eminently worth sampling firsthand.

ACCOMMODATIONS AND MEALS

Many come to Swans just for the day, but, if you plan to stay over, the **Harbor Watch Motel and Bikes** in Minturn is open throughout the year and offers accommodations more or less in the middle of the rangy island. The Harbor Watch also rents bicycles, which are an excellent way of getting around this island. Call ahead, especially in summer: (207) 526-4563 or (800) 532-7928.

The **Harborside Market** in Swans Island Village offers sandwiches, groceries, and film. The **General Store** in Minturn has a luncheonette, and also sells groceries. Both are generally open year-round, though the General store had a fire in July 2005. As this book goes to press, the word is that the store will reopen in fall 2005.

GETTING THERE

Maine State Ferry Service to Swans on the *Captain Henry Lee* departs from Bass Harbor at the extreme southwest corner of Mount Desert Island. Local information on these trips can be had by calling the local Maine State Ferry Service office at (207) 244-3254 during business hours. There are multiple trips daily to Swans Island year-round from Bass Harbor. When purchasing your ticket, be sure to reserve space on a specific return trip if you are transporting a vehicle. On summer weekends, space for vehicles going to or coming from Swans is taken up quickly. Going out on the first run and coming back midafternoon, rather than waiting for the last return trip, is advisable if you are transporting a car.

Twenty-four-hour on-call air service is available to Swans via **Penobscot Island Air** at Knox County Airport, Owls Head, four miles south of US 1 and Rockland, tel. (207) 596-7500.

Gulf of Maine

FRENCHBORO (LONG ISLAND)

Frenchboro is Long Island's sole community, a village served by a single road with a spur or two, the quintessential island outpost dedicated to fishing. A roundish mound about two and a half miles across, Long looks outward toward the open Atlantic and the Gulf of Maine a modest distance below Placentia and Black Islands. With Swans away to the west, this whole cluster of isles rests due south of Mount Desert. Frenchboro supports approximately sixty souls, and then a bit more in summer, all dwelling around the isle's protected harbor along its west side. It has that feeling of smallness and separateness appropriate to a community whose position at sea determines much. One might say that Frenchboro is one of few examples of coastal island life where fishing occupations continue largely undisturbed, and where community life has not been shaped by tourism.

Some would claim there are more deer than humans on this island, the whitetails being tame enough to eat from the hands of those they trust. These deer shelter in Long's thick coniferous woods, which are largely owned by the David Rockefeller heirs. Most of the island's twenty-five hundred or so acres have been preserved in a pristine state with few signs of development, and the island has, thus, maintained its character as a small fishing outland unspoiled by the usual hokum artifices of modernity.

Long was originally part of that seaward cluster known as the Burnt Coat Islands, all of which belonged to Colonel Swan. It later passed by default to Michael O'Maley, who sold individual parcels here to island families in the years 1823 to 1835, even as Swan himself languished in a Paris debtors' prison. Israel Lunt built a store on the island in 1822, and by 1835 owned nearly half of Long, more than eleven hundred acres, all purchased for the munificent sum of about eight hundred dollars. The community was formally recognized as Long Island Plantation by the state in 1840, and Frenchboro acquired its post office in 1850, naming itself after its influential benefactor, attorney E. Webster French. The island's population peaked in 1910 at 197 residents, with as many as sixty children enrolled in its two-room schoolhouse. The number of scholars had dropped to as few as eight in the mid-1980s. Today, if you work here, you are likely to fish for lobster in season and do a bit of scalloping in the off-season months.

Long Island has struggled to maintain itself as a

Frenchboro (Long Island)

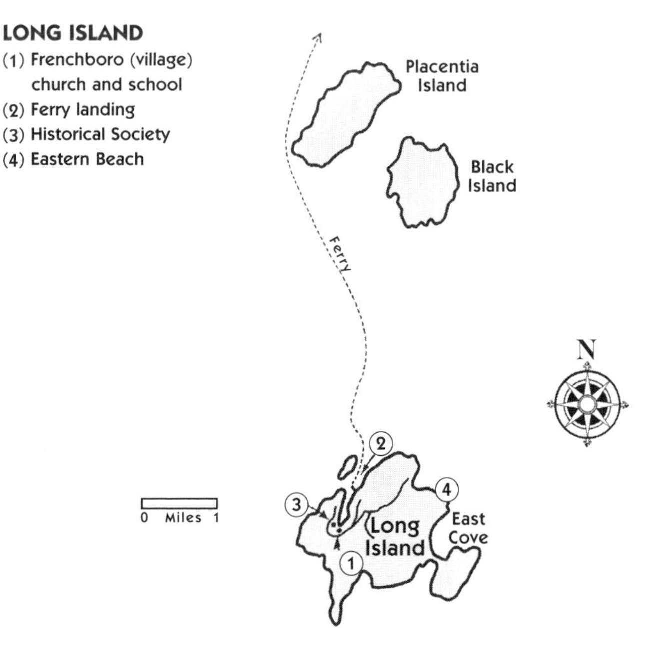

viable community, a problem confronting several offshore isles that have not taken their place in the vacation homes circuit. A number of years back, islanders invited families with children and essential skills to move to Frenchboro in an effort to maintain a critical population mass on the island and to keep the school open. Ads were run in a number of national newspapers and magazines inviting applicants, who were offered attractive housing loans and other supports. Of that small number who passed the rigorous vetting process, a few moved to the island; even fewer stayed for the long term. Many are attracted to island life, but, of those who will stay all year, the numbers are very small.

In the 1960s, with only two children at school, islanders invited fourteen mainland children to board with them and go to classes on the island, which saved their school from state closure. Telephone service came to Frenchboro in 1982 to the relief of most islanders, and power has come via cable from nearby Swans Island since the 1950s. Fresh water in Frenchboro is drawn from deep wells dug in the rock underlayment. This is the extent of Frenchboro's willing participation in the encumbrances of the twenty-first century.

Paying a visit to Frenchboro and returning to the mainland on the same day is possible from Mount Desert's Bass Harbor, but requires some forethought. Day-visitors should plan to travel *on Fridays* from April through November. (See Getting There, below.) Those coming to the island will enjoy a stroll out the

path to pretty Eastern Beach, a shingle strand of killick stones worked by the tide. Other trails lead to Eastern, Western, and Deep Coves. The untrammeled woods of Long Island are exceptionally attractive. Frenchboro also boasts a small museum with information on island life and history. No accommodations or meal service were available on Long Island in 2005, but some islanders will occasionally take in an overnight guest. Inquire in the village. Camping and campfires are not allowed on the island. Please respect private property and carry any trash you bring back to the mainland.

GETTING THERE

Maine State Ferry Service to Frenchboro on the *Captain Henry Lee* departs from Bass Harbor at the extreme southwest corner of Mount Desert Island. Local information on these trips can be had by calling the Maine State Ferry Service local office at (207) 244-3254 during business hours.

A single round trip to Frenchboro departs on Wednesdays, Thursdays, and Sundays year-round, but does not pause at the island except to load. Summer day-visitors to Frenchboro should plan to take the *Captain Henry Lee* from Bass Harbor on a Friday at 8 A.M. and return to the mainland on a second ferry trip at 6 P.M. from Frenchboro. (This twice-a-day Friday service operates from April through November. In November, return service leaves Frenchboro at 5 P.M.)

Gulf of Maine

THE CRANBERRY ISLES

Offshore places sometimes take their names from eccentricities of landscape, and this cluster of islands honors that rule. A sprawling cranberry bog of some two hundred acres greeted early arrivals to

Wharf at Great Cranberry

Cranberry Isles

GREAT CRANBERRY ISLAND

(1) Ferry landing
(2) Rusty Anchor Takeout
(3) Cafe and general store
(4) School
(5) Boatyard
(6) Fish Point
(7) "The Pool" (Fish Cove)

ISLESFORD VILLAGE, LITTLE CRANBERRY ISLAND

(1) Ferry landing; Islesford Museum
(2) Post office and Islesford Market
(3) Graves of first settlers, 1769
(4) Old Coast Guard Station (private)
(5) Church
(6) Islesford Dock Restaurant
(7) Island Bed & Breakfast

BAKER ISLAND

(1) Lighthouse
(2) Landing Beach
(3) "Dance Floor"
Acadia National Park

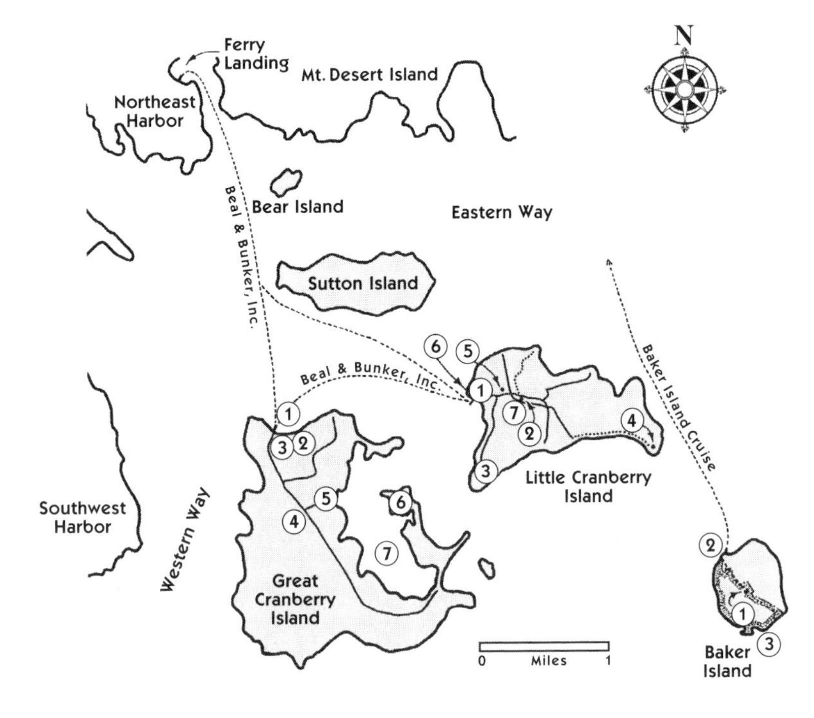

the largest island here, and the entire group—Great Cranberry, Little Cranberry, Baker, and Sutton—were all soon known as simply "the Cranberries." Along with tiny Bear Island, this collection of outposts was, in 1830, formally recognized by the recently minted Maine legislature as Cranberry Isles Township. This very attractive fivesome lies close to Mount Desert Island off Southwest Harbor and has known human visitation since well before the first landing of Europeans in the region.

The Cranberries appear to have been in the center of early coastal exploration, ships from many European nations from Spain to Scandinavia sailing betwixt and around the group as they headed for welcoming Somes Sound on Mount Desert. Samuel de Champlain may have landed on Great Cranberry as he coasted Mount Desert during a kind of mapping expedition in 1604. The French cleric Father Briard was among the small group who set up housekeeping by a perpetual spring on the west side of Somes Sound in 1613. Briard is likely to have explored the Isles before his little community was routed by the English and sent packing.

In September 1759, London came into full possession of the New England coast with the fall of Quebec. The coast and islands of this region were conveyed to Massachusetts, with part of Mount Desert and all of the nearby islands reserved to Marie Thérèse de la Mothe Cadillac de Gregoire, granddaughter of the first *Seigneur des Mont Deserts*. Her lands were soon sold, and families such as the Stanleys, Spurlings, and Bunkers became Great Cranberry settlers. Led by Benjamin Spurling, who had come north from Portsmouth, New Hampshire, the settlers were from the start anti-Tory and given to revolt. They would have occasion in the new century to give the British a spanking.

Gradually, this cluster of islands was occupied by hardy types willing to brave the risks of coming north, leaving behind more settled communities in southern New England. Job Stanley ventured to Little Cranberry in 1760, but remained only briefly. Benjamin Bunker followed him to the Isles in 1762. John Stanley came aboard in 1769. The Gilley family, out of Newburyport, resided at Baker Island during the early 1800s. William Gilley and his wife, Hannah, were known for their self-reliance, building their homestead on Baker from nothing and raising a family of twelve. William Gilley became keeper of the light here.

The Hadlock family on Little Cranberry built their fortunes at sea and as merchants. Hadlocks became shipbuilders, too, and lost many of their kin at sea. Their descendants are still active today as merchants at Islesford. Eben Sutton came into possession of the island named after him at the cost of two quarts of rum, but the island was first occupied in 1854 by John Gilley and his wife Harriett, who purchased a fifty-acre plot there. Gilley, with his second wife, later became an able merchant selling the products of his farming to new arrivals on Mount Desert. John Gilley was said to have rowed his dory full of produce, eggs, and milk to Northeast Harbor faithfully each day for many years, but he disappeared in October 1896 when a sudden storm apparently took his boat and drowned him in the channel.

During the War of 1812, the British forced the islanders to pay tribute or see their ships and property taken or burned. Officers of the British sloop *Tenedos* demanded $350 from Captain Spurling not to burn ships the family had hidden in Somes Sound. When the family refused, the British came menacingly into Norwoods Cove aboard two armed barges, unaware that islanders had rallied and lay in wait to resist them. Led by Robert Spurling, the

Boarding at Islesford, Little Cranberry

islanders fired at the Englishmen from the shelter of the woods, killing seven of them and sending the *Tenedos* scurrying.

Great Cranberry is the largest of the Isles, running to two miles in length and a mile in width. The island's 490 acres support a year-round community of about a hundred persons, which grows 400 to 500 percent in summer. There is a small commercial district around Spurling Cove by the ferry wharf on Great Cranberry's northwest corner. A central road connects the north and south of the island. Great Cranberry is shaped like an enormous, open lobster claw. At the tip of the claw is Fish Point, site of earlier efforts to dry fish on the island. Between the point and the rest of the landmass is Fish Cove, or simply "The Pool," a natural protected harbor. There is a summer take-out food service and a year-round general store on the island.

Acadia National Park maintains a museum on Little Cranberry, a 350-acre island community just east of Great Cranberry. The Islesford Museum, open in summer, features sea and shore memorabilia, historic papers, traditional tools, ship models, and other relics of island life. Haverford College professor William Otis Sawtelle founded this collection in an attractive brick structure in 1927. Island shops featuring locally produced crafts are located nearby. Islesford is Little Cranberry's main center and is host to the fishing cooperative and the lobster and fishing fleet that lands catch here. The island has a seasonal bed-and-breakfast and summer restaurant.

At low tide, you can walk across the sandbar from Little Cranberry to Baker Island, but unless you know all the vagaries of local tides and currents, it is better (and safer) to sail from Northeast Harbor to Baker. Islesford Ferry provides a guided trip to the island, an island walk with a naturalist-guide, and the ride back to the mainland twice daily in summer. Baker has no dock facilities, so visitors on this trip are rowed ashore in traditional dories. The lighthouse first manned by William Gilley still stands here and is visited on the walking tour.

MEALS AND ACCOMMODATIONS

On Great Cranberry, **Seawich Cafe & Cranberry General Store** has beverages and sandwich fixings (207) 244-5336. **Rusty Anchor Takeout** offers chowders and sandwiches at picnic tables (207) 244-3900.

On Little Cranberry, the **Islesford Dock Restaurant** provides three meals daily, and offers sandwiches and ice cream at a take-out window with picnic table seating (207) 244-7494. The year-round **Islesford Market** vends a variety of sandwich fixings and snacks (207) 244-7667.

Lodging is available on Little Cranberry at **Island Bed and Breakfast** in Islesford.

For those arriving on their own boats, there are rental moorings by the **Islesford Dock Restaurant** on Little Cranberry; water, gasoline, and diesel are available at the fisherman's co-op dock near the ferry landing. On Great Cranberry Island, **Beal and Bunker, Inc.,** sells gasoline and diesel. The **Cranberry Island Boatyard** does repairs and offers yacht storage.

GETTING THERE

The Cranberry Isles are reached several times daily by **Beal and Bunker** from Northeast Harbor on Mount Desert Island. Their boat *Sea Queen* makes a twenty-minute run to both Little and Great Cranberry. The boat offers four trips daily and three on Sunday throughout the year, increasing to six trips daily in the high season. Beal and Bunker also runs historic tours to Islesford on Little Cranberry seasonally. For schedules and information, call (207) 244-3575.

The **Baker Island Cruise Boat** departs Northeast Harbor for the island with seasonal excursions from June through September. Contact the **Islesford Ferry** at (207) 276-3717 during normal business hours. The Cranberry Isles are also served by **Great Harbor Tours** on the *Elizabeth T* out of Southwest Harbor. Contact Captain Storey King at (207) 460-5200. Cranberry Isles trips and charters are offered seasonally by **Cranberry Cove Boating** in Southwest Harbor at (207) 244-5882, as are trips by Captain John Dwelley at **Delight Water Taxi**, tel. (207) 244-5724.

Enjoying Maine's Islands

ENVIRONMENTAL PROGRAMS AND VACATIONS ON MAINE ISLANDS

Those who value both islands and learning will find much of interest in summer island camps and seminars focused on the natural world offshore in Maine. Programs study wildlife, avian life, and marine biology, and also train participants in self-reliance and leadership. Leading programs are based at shoreline preserves or at sea, and attendees get to not only engage in a superb learning experience but also sample island life firsthand.

The largest variety of island environmental offerings is provided by **Maine Audubon**, whose **Hog Island Camp** in Bremen launches a full slate of interesting courses each year. Field ornithology, coastal natural history, educators' workshops, seabird study, and kayak trips are typical fare. There are also courses designed particularly for families, children, and teenagers. As the Maine Audubon program guide says, "Accessible only by boat, Hog

Island Audubon Camp is nestled in a 330-acre coastal wildlife sanctuary in Bremen, Maine. Since 1936, its summer programs for adults, educators, young people and families have been led by some of the most respected naturalists and environmental educators in the nation." The camp's locus on the lip of Muscongus Bay makes this an outstanding place to learn about Maine's unique saltwater environments. For information and to register, call (888) 325-5261 or e-mail: camps@maineaudubon.org. Information is also on the Maine Audubon Web site at www. maineaudubon.org.

A source of information on activities, programs, and events tied to island life is the **Island Institute**, publisher of the outstanding annual *Island Journal*. The institute is concerned with supporting and improving the island way of life, resource management, and education. Its offices and store are on Main Street in Rockland, not far from the ferry landing. The Island Institute, P.O. Box 429, Rockland, ME 04841, tel. (800) 339-9209, or (207) 594-9209.

West of Vinalhaven is the **Hurricane Island Outward Bound School**, a major center for ocean-connected training since 1948. This experientially based program, a part of the worldwide Outward Bound network, is focused on personal development, survival skills, team building, and self-reliance through challenging days at sea, using the island as base. The **Maine Sea Program** at Hurricane takes course members to a variety of islands in thirty-foot, ketch-rigged pulling boats while they learn navigation, seamanship, and sailing skills. Course participants solo by spending three days alone on a remote island to test their practical survival skills, and members also acquire rock climbing ability in the island's rock quarries. Natural history and other courses are offered. Contact: Hurricane Island Outward Bound School, P.O. Box 429, Rockland, ME 04841, tel. (866) 746-9771.

For campers and kayakers who like to do their island bedding down out-of-doors, the **Appalachian Mountain Club** operates its **Beal Island Campsite** in Georgetown, Maine. This primitive island camping place is open to club members and friends, and is an excellent destination for persons island-hopping in Hockamock and Montsweag Bays. (See the author's *Rivers of Memory*.) Kayakers can put in at Knubble Bay Camp in Georgetown or elsewhere in the bays. Contact the Appalachian Mountain Club, 5 Joy Street, Boston, MA 02108, tel. (617) 523-0636, for information and membership.

The **Maine Island Trail Association** has linked together a series of offshore islands where kayakers may come ashore, rest and picnic, and, in some cases, camp. Routes have been mapped, rules and regulations printed and distributed, and owner permissions to land secured. The complete trail carries kayakers and boaters along 325 miles of coastline. The island trail network visits a number of isles not usually seen by the hordes, and can provide a primal, natural experience for the skilled kayaker.

Recently, some islands have begun to show

signs of careless and detrimental use, particularly by powerboaters who seem to view these outposts as toilets and beer can repositories. If you tour by powerboat, sail, or cruise the islands in a kayak, please respect the environmental fragility of those islands you visit, and remove all trash. Most islands are privately owned, and continued access depends upon respectful use.

Information on the trail can be found in sporting goods stores, in libraries, and through associations such as Maine Audubon or the Sierra Club of Maine. See also the Maine Island Trail Web site (www.info @mita.org). Memberships are available to support this worthy program. Contact Maine Island Trail Association, Suite 30-3, 58 Fore Street, Portland, ME 04101, tel. (207) 761-8225.